Charles Elliot R.N.
1801-1875

A SERVANT OF BRITAIN OVERSEAS

by
CLAGETTE BLAKE

LONDON · CLEAVER-HUME PRESS LTD

CLEAVER-HUME PRESS LIMITED
31 *Wright's Lane, London W 8*

© CLAGETTE BLAKE 1960

First published 1960

Crown 4to, xvi+130 *pp.*
11 *plates*
Library of Congress
Catalogue Card Number
60–15573

Printed in Great Britain by
HUGH PATON & SONS LTD, EDINBURGH

Acknowledgements

In the writing of this book, my debts have become legion. Grateful acknowledgement is due to many; at the University of Texas: to Professors Eugene Campbell Barker, Milton Rietow Gutsch, Walter Prescott Webb, Thad Riker, Frederick Duncalf, Caleb Perry Patterson, Charles Flynn Arrowood, Hob Gray, William James Battle, Hanson Tufts Parlin and William Henry Harper; to the University of Texas Library staff; to the Texas State Library staff; to Professor Newton Edwards, University of South Carolina; to Professor William Campbell Binkley, Tulane University; to the Library of Congress and Microfilm and Map Divisions' staffs, Washington D C; to Mr Foster Vance Phipps Jr, Washington D C; to Mr John Lester Sims, San Antonio; in England: to Professors William Norton Medlicott and W. G. Beasley, University of London; to Mr Maurice Collis, British Civil Service official and author; to Messrs W. J. Keswick, Matheson and Company Ltd, and C. V. Hill, Librarian, The Admiralty, and to the Public Record Office and University of London Library staffs; to His Excellency Sir Hubert Rance, Governor of Trinidad, for the photograph of Charles Elliot; to Messrs P. J. Edmonds, J. L. Robson, and the entire Cleaver-Hume publishing staff and to the Printers, Hugh Paton and Sons Ltd, Edinburgh, for their care in the final production of the book.

CLAGETTE BLAKE

Saint Anthony's Town, April 1960

Contents

ERRATA

Page 62, line 25 : *for* William Hanry Low *read* William Henry Low.
Page 99, line 10 : *for* Washington-on-the-Beazos *read* Washington-on-the-Brazos.
Page 112, line 23 : *for* 1947 *read* 1847.
Page 118, line 34 : *for* 15b *read* 13b.
Page 123, line 7 : *for* Helens's *read* Helena's.

List of Illustrations

Such garbled memories upon Fame's fragile page.
        —Gilbert Emery, *The Power and the Glory*.

Introduction

AMONG the myriad of figures met in my native state's history, that of Charles Elliot intrigues me. He appeared as chargé d'affaires and conducted British interests and activities in the Republic of Texas, 1842-46, fought annexation and lost. The man seemed obscured by the magnitude of events to which Britain had assigned him, even before the Texas mission. He had never been the subject of biographical study, and this book aims to show the light such a figure throws on the varied nature of British commitments and on the type of men Britain chose to authorize to undertake them.

19th-century England found ways and means of adjusting her own special pattern of economic interests to the wider world pattern. During most of the century, she enjoyed the benefits of freedom from major European wars, and these years of extraordinary peace were ones in which the effects of the Industrial Revolution, of Wesleyanism, the French Revolution and the Napoleonic Wars were working themselves out. Elliot's century was a changing century and the forces of change were amazing: it was the age of the philanthropists and partisan reformers; of Britain's assertion, for 50 years after Waterloo, as the exemplar and pattern of free constitutional government and of numerous and varied constitutional and political reforms; of the abolition of slavery—both transportation and institution; of great economic and social reforms; of the assertion of Britain's great technological lead in industry and the growth of her vast merchant navy; it was the age of free trade and materialism on one hand and of generous humanitarianism on the other. After 1815, the British Navy suffered eclipse in popularity and the Army held the stage until the Crimean War and the growth of armaments in other European states caused England to realize that the fleet was the determining factor in her whole position, both in Europe and as a maritime Empire, and as the framework for her policy of free trade to ensure for all the freedom of the seas.

It was this policy which led England to taking a firm stand in the China question where, from 1836 to August 1841, Elliot alone directed, as the Crown's chief administrator in China, affairs of the first magnitude. The Opium War broke out in 1840 and Elliot ordered the surrender of four millions sterling of opium, admitted Canton to ransom, secured Hong Kong for the Empire, won the diplomatic victory of stating publicly what came to be known as the Open Door, and was defended by Macaulay in Parliament. These China affairs amounted as it were to the entry of Western energies and ideas into forbidden China, into the Ancient and Far East's very heart, an entry fatal in the end to the Great Pure Dynasty and an entry which enabled Westerners to dominate Far Eastern markets for many generations. A century and four months after Elliot retired from China, the Japanese counter-attacked this Western mastery.

Elliot, cognizant that the British must ply their trade and that the Empire must always regard the element of strategical necessity, went out to the fledgling Republic of Texas. There, as perhaps nowhere else, Elliot's engaging dual personality, that of the political dreamer and that of the sincere philanthropist, manifested itself. Always, a healthy English patriotism underlay his every action, yet mixed and conflicting motives actuated the man. He was a genuine Victorian theoretical philanthropist in his desire to better the condition of the coloured race which, in his youthful and active navy days, he had first seen downtrodden on the West African slave coast. Then, years later, as their Protector in Guiana, he had taken the black man's side and, consequently, been called home to advise the Government, then about to abolish slavery, on the West Indian question. Yet these moral sentiments did not necessarily conflict with his ideas of national profit. He was a spirited opponent of American expansion and desired that England assume a position on the American continent that would block further territorial advance of the United States. At home, he sympathized with the majority of Parliament which voted against a reduction of sugar duties, on the reasoning that reduction of those duties would encourage the institution of slavery. At the same time, not only Elliot but every English traveller and writer who visited America between 1835 and 1845 was appalled at the growth of the United States and expressed fear and apprehension upon the future power of America. Elliot's personal and official letters attest the same and haunting fear. Also, to Elliot as to every Britisher, the independent Republic idea had strong appeal.

Elliot, a man blessed with aristocracy of talent and birth, a man of intense experience and forceful reactions, can be forgiven the laborious effort involved in deciphering his illegible penmanship. His letters and reports, both private and official, often tinged with a classic British acidity and supreme understatement, yield valuable and interesting contemporary information and pen-portraits of imperial and local conditions wherever he was stationed during the half century he served the Royal Navy and the Colonial and Foreign Offices. The mind that impelled the pen was one of extraordinary penetration. Elliot was well educated and informed, enjoyed the company of thinkers, was intimate with the leaders and with the common man, and was deeply absorbed in the remarkably widening and changing world of his century. He was, too, of an artistic nature and his drawings and water-colours, particularly those of the Far East's captivating ports and scenes, are said to be both well composed and topographically most informing.

19th-century England found her historian in Macaulay, her poet laureate in Tennyson, and her statesmen in Palmerston, Gladstone, and Disraeli. In Charles Elliot, one of a company whose names are legion, she found an active agent who was prepared to spend the greater part of his life away from his homeland—a loyal servant in the building up and sustaining of a maritime Empire in a changing world.

Early Years

————⦅⦆————

THE name of Elliot is one of the most ancient and distinguished on the Scottish border. The Elliots came to Scotland towards the close of the 14th century; much of their family history has been lost in the burning of various writs and documents by the great fire which took place at Stobs, one of the clan's seats, about the middle of the 18th century.[5a] One of the greatest of the early Elliots, and the founder of the family's good fortune, was Sir Gilbert Elliot (1651-1718), later Lord Minto, and popularly known as Gibbie Elliot, writer and advocate.

But Charles Elliot was to see little of his Scottish homeland in his long and devoted career in the Public Service. He was born in 1801, son to Hugh Elliot, H.M.'s diplomatic representative stationed at Dresden. The early years of his life passed rapidly, and in many locales, where he was able to profit from the opportunities which his father's career and family connections offered. But already, the background of late 18th century Britain was changing, and his career in public service was to be very different from that of his father's—affected as it was, at home, by patronage and powerful families, and abroad by the threat of a Europe dominated by France.

Charles Elliot's grandfather, first Earl Minto, had his two sons, Gilbert and Hugh, educated first under tutors at home in Scotland and then, from 1764 to 1766, at the Abbé Choquant's school in Paris. There Hugh struck up what was to be a lifelong friendship with his fellow-pupil, the great Mirabeau; and there, at the Abbé's school, David Hume acted as guardian for the young Scots as they studied away from home. In 1768, the Elliot boys were sent as gentlemen commoners to Christ Church, Oxford, and, after two years, years which seem to have been occupied chiefly with the pursuit of sport and society, Gilbert went on to study law and was in Parliament by 1774. There, he early gave proof of his talents both as a debater and as a man of business practicality. His record in Parliament, during the American and French revolutions and especially his services in aid to the French royalist refugees, prompted George III to acknowledge his sense of Sir Gilbert's services to the Crown, both on the Continent and afield, by raising him to the peerage under the title of Baron of Minto, in the shire of Roxburgh, with a special permission to adopt the arms of Corsica into the armorial bearings of his family.

Meanwhile, Hugh had gone to the famous military school at Metz. In 1771, Hugh's longing after a military career was checked by the refusal of Lord Barrington, then Secretary of War, to confirm the commission which had been granted to him as a child. This was a severe blow to Elliot's ambitions and, being foiled at home, he went to Vienna in the hope of getting a commission in the Austrian service. In this also he was unsuccessful but he determined to see war and served as a volunteer with the Russian army in the campaign of 1772 against the Turks. In this war, in the words of Romanzow, the Russian general, 'Hugh Elliot distinguished himself by a truly British courage'.

Then, aided by the influence of his father in Parliament, Hugh secured a diplomatic appointment. In 1773, when but one-and-twenty, he was appointed minister plenipotentiary at Munich and, in 1775, representative of the kingdom of Hanover at the diet of Ratisbon as well. But Hugh Elliot was discontented and, in 1776, he threw up this post and returned to England for a time. Once again did his father and elder brother, both in Parliament by now, and both, though Whigs, active in the prosecution of the American war, exert their influence in his behalf. In April 1777, he was sent to Berlin as envoy extraordinary and minister plenipotentiary to the court of Prussia; in 1782, he was transferred to Copenhagen.

Hugh Elliot remained in Denmark for nine years, years of great importance in the history of Denmark and years which, at long last, firmly established the Elliot name as belonging to men of diplomatic repute. In Copenhagen, Elliot had every need to exercise his powers for the King of Denmark, in spite of his relationship to George III, was by no means well disposed towards England, and it was only with difficulty that Elliot could carry out the policy of his close friend, England's prime minister. The astute William Pitt was, during these times of revolution in France, aiming to keep Denmark in a close political alliance with England in order to counteract the growing power of Russia in the Baltic. In 1791, Pitt, pleased with Elliot's success in Denmark, called the diplomat home for talk and very soon he sent him on a most secret mission to Paris. The details of the plan appear almost certainly intended to win over the support of Elliot's intimate friend and correspondent, Mirabeau, then the leading statesman of the French assembly. After repeating his successful Danish diplomacy once again in Paris, Hugh Elliot received appointment as minister pleni-

2

potentiary to Dresden, and remained in the court of Saxony until 1803.[6a] While at Dresden, his son Charles Elliot was born.

The Countess of Minto, in *Hugh Elliot's Memoir*, records of her grandfather's Dresden post:

> . . . Revolutionised France had started into life with a giant's strength prepared to use it like a giant. And during the ten years passed by Mr Elliot in Saxony, his correspondence is occupied with details concerning the submissions of small powers, the struggles of great ones, the intrigues of French emigrants, and the insolence of French agents. A voluminous correspondence with his brother, after the latter had become Lord Minto and Envoy to Vienna, contains very little matter of public interest at the present date. One short note, however, has a trait in which we see that time and circumstances had not entirely subdued early predilections in the diplomatist's breast. 'Suwarrow',[1] he said, 'is at Prague; if it were not for my family ties, I should be strongly tempted to throw up my post and have a campaign with my old chief'. A quarter of a century before he had written from Munich, his first diplomatic post, 'My greatest pleasure is to shut my eyes and fancy myself in Count Woronzow's tent on the Danube'.[6b]

Lord Minto, on his way to Vienna as envoy extraordinary, visited his brother Hugh in Dresden and wrote to his wife in England letters which afford an intimate glimpse into the lives of Charles' parents. Some years had passed since the brothers had met and, in the interval, Hugh Elliot, wrote Gilbert, had married 'a beautiful girl of humble birth, but whose personal qualities justified his choice'.[6c] Lord Minto, continuing his letter to his wife from Dresden, said:

> I have, since I have seen Hugh's wife and beautiful children, better hope of his happiness than I ever had before. She is very handsome—her face and head remarkably pretty, in so much that the celebrated Virgin of Raphael in the gallery, one of the finest pictures I ever saw, is her exact portrait; while two of the children are so like the cherubs looking up that I told Hugh it was a family picture. I find her sensible and pleasant, and they are both generally liked, and on the best possible footing here.
>
> Hugh's extreme good humour and temper, and his affectionate and cordial manner to every creature that approaches him, in whatever shape, are captivating qualities.[6c]

Soon after this writing, it was Lady Minto's turn to write to her husband of the household at Dresden and her letter is no less cordial than Lord Minto's. She wrote:

> I am delighted with Dresden, with the gallery . . . with the country, in which there seems so much comfort and so many beautiful scenes. We take long airings every evening, and I know you will be glad to hear that I admire Mrs Elliot and the children to the utmost.

1 Hugh Elliot was attached to General Suwarrow's staff when the latter took and destroyed the town of Turticaya and was the messenger dispatched by Suwarrow with the news to General Romanzow.

After glowing tribute to Margaret Elliot's uncommon beauty and pleasing manner, Lady Minto ended her letter thus: 'The children are really charming, and the two groups are hugging and kissing, and intimate friends already'.[6c]

After these family reunions in Dresden, Lord Minto, writing to his brother, confided, 'It is a happiness to me that for a moment our families have made one family'.[6c]

The Elliots were at the court of Saxony until 1803, when Sir Hugh was transferred to Naples. At the new post, the English family struck up a warm friendship with the Queen, sister of Marie Antoinette and former friend of the Lady Hamilton. It was not long before Sir Hugh had come so far under the charming Queen's influence that he deserted the hard lessons learned in the many courts of Europe—courts where he had served his own King so well. Angrily, and in downright unEnglish fashion, did Elliot forbid Sir James Henry Craig, newly come to Naples at the head of an English army, to leave Naples. Craig was shocked and hesitated. Then, Elliot ordered him to defend the Neapolitan dominions in Italy and Craig wisely refused and took his army to Sicily, whither the King and Queen of Naples speedily fled. Elliot was recalled from his post.

The years 1803 to 1809 were almost the only years, until he was an old man, in which the young boy, Charles, was to know his native isles. These six years soon passed with tutors and in the company of both the Scottish and the English Elliots. The government decided not to employ his father again in diplomacy after his behaviour at Naples; but they could not long neglect the brother of the powerful and influential Earl of Minto. For distinguished services as Governor-General of India, during which office he accompanied in person the successful expedition against Java in 1811, Gilbert Elliot had received the thanks of Parliament and, in February 1813, was created Earl of Minto and Viscount Melgund. In 1809, Hugh Elliot was appointed Governor of the Leeward Islands.

The condition of the Continent—from which the success of Bonaparte's armies had all but banished diplomacy—and the risks and expenses consequent on the removal of a family from place to place, had decided Hugh Elliot to abandon a diplomatic for a less brilliant, but also a less precarious, career. But it was at great sacrifice of personal happiness that he accepted an assignment in the far-distant clime of the West Indies to which he felt it impossible that his family should accompany him. The next five years were lonely ones spent at a post where accounts of the cruelties practised upon the slave population filled his letters home.[6d]

In 1814, Hugh Elliot was recalled from the Leeward Islands, sworn a member of His Majesty's Privy Council, and made Governor of Madras.[6e] In India, Sir Hugh and all his family, with the exception of two boys left at home in school, lived until 1820 when they returned to England. There he lived in retirement until his death, 2nd December 1830;[11] he was buried by the side of his beloved brother in Westminster Abbey.[6f]

Charles Elliot, one of the boys left at school in England in 1814, early succumbed to the lure of the sea. He entered the navy and, when but fourteen, put to sea, 26th March 1815, as First-class Volunteer on board the *Leviathan*. His skipper was Captain Thomas Briggs, whose station was the Mediterranean.[7a]

So began Charles Elliot's long career of public service. Although not one of the great or conspicuous figures of the 19th century, his career does show the varied and far-flung nature of British commitments in the 19th century, and throws invaluable light on the men on whom she relied to carry out the decisions of the Home Government, and on whose shoulders she placed the day-to-day administration of the Empire.

BIBLIOGRAPHY & REFERENCES

MICROFILM

1 *Public Record Office Lists and Indexes, No. XVIII, List of Admiralty Records*. London: Printed for His Majesty's Stationery Office by Mackie and Company, Ltd., 1904. Loaned by John Crerar Library, Chicago.

OTHER MATERIALS

2 Letters (1950-52): C. V. Hill, Librarian, The Admiralty, Whitehall, to Clagette Blake.

PRINTED

3 Anderson, William, *The Scottish Nation; or, The Surnames, Families, Literature, Honours, and Biographical History of the People of Scotland*, Vol. II. Edinburgh: A. Fulbarton and Co., 1875.

4 Burke, John Bernard, *A Genealogical and Heraldic Dictionary of the Peerages of England, Ireland, and Scotland*. London: H. Colburn, 1846.

5 Carré, Walter Riddell, *Border Memories; or Sketches of Prominent Men and Women of the Border*. Edited by James Tait. Edinburgh: James Thin, 1876. Loaned by The University of Cincinnati Library.
   a p.139.

6 Minto, Countess of, *A Memoir of the Right Honourable Hugh Elliot*. Edinburgh: Edmonston and Douglas, 1868. Loaned by the University of Michigan.
   a p.335; *b* p.336; *c* p.338; *d* pp.403-11; *e* p.411; *f* pp.411-15.

11 Hugh Elliot's surviving children at the time of his death were five sons and three daughters: Henry, Lieutenant-Colonel in the Army, died in 1842; Edward, for many years Police Magistrate at Madras, died in 1866; Gilbert Elliot was Dean of Bristol; Charles Elliot, of whom this writing is a study; Frederick, Assistant Under-Secretary of State for the Colonial Department; Emma, died in 1866; Harriet Agnes, died in 1845; Caroline, god-daughter of the Queen of Naples. Hugh Elliot's daughter by a first marriage, Isabella, married at Dresden in 1801 to George Payne, Esquire, died in 1826; a son by his second marriage, Maximilian, died in India in the same year.

7 O'Byrne, William R., *A Naval Biographical Dictionary: comprising the Life and Services of Every Living Officer in Her Majesty's Navy, from the Rank of Admiral of the Fleet to that of Lieutenant, inclusive. Compiled from Authentic and Family Documents*. London: John Murray, Publisher to the Admiralty, 1849. Loaned by The Library of Congress. (A letter from C. V. Hill, Librarian at the Admiralty, Whitehall, 20.6.1950, to Clagette Blake states that the Admiralty accepts O'Byrne's accounts of the services of Admiral Sir Charles Elliot as authoritative.)
   a p.332.
8 *Webster's Biographical Dictionary*. 1st ed., Article, 'Elliot'. Springfield, Massachusetts: G. and C. Merriam and Co., 1948.

The Sea

ABOARD the *Leviathan* the young seaman, Charles Elliot, began his naval schooling on the great highways of the sea and got his sea legs on the Lisbon, Cork and Mediterranean stations.[3a] Then came duty under fire.

During the colossal wars of which Europe was the scene between 1793 and 1815, the Moorish pirates, particularly those of Algiers, carried on their depredations with comparative impunity. Although St Vincent and even Nelson himself checked their activities on several occasions, and the American Commodore Stephen Decatur taught them a sharp lesson immediately after the conclusion of peace between Great Britain and the United States, the pirates still ravaged the Mediterranean shores. In 1816, after renewed outrages and vain negotiations, a formidable British expedition was organized to bring the Dey of Algiers to reason. Admiral Lord Exmouth was entrusted with the command and Charles Elliot, then but fifteen, was made a midshipman on the *Minden*, a 74-gun vessel under the command of Captain William Paterson.

The British fleet of 19 vessels sailed from Plymouth on 28th July and, upon arriving at Gibraltar on 9th August, found there a six-vessel Dutch squadron, the commander of which asked and obtained leave to co-operate with Exmouth in the contemplated action. On 14th August, after brief delay caused by adverse winds, the combined fleet weighed. Two days out from Gibraltar, it was met by the *Prometheus*, under Commander William Bateman Dashwood, directly out of Algiers, with fugitives and with the information that part of her crew and the British Consul, Mr McDonell, had been detained by the Moors. Having to beat windward for some days, the fleet did not make Cape Cazzina until the 26th, and did not sight Algiers till the early morning of the 27th, when the sea was very nearly calm. Demands for the release of Christian slaves, repayment of money which recently had been paid for the freeing of slaves, peace with the Netherlands, and liberation of both the British Consul and the *Prometheus's* people, were immediately sent in by Lieutenant Samuel Burgess. Meanwhile, the fleet stood on slowly with a light sea breeze, and at length lay to about a mile from the city. In mid-afternoon, Burgess returned without the reply which the Moors had promised should be given within two hours. Admiral Lord Exmouth thereupon asked by signal whether all his ships, British and Dutch, were ready and, the affirmative flag being instantly hoisted by every vessel, he bore up to the attack against the powerful defences of Algiers with his entire fleet.

The total number of guns in the Moorish batteries has been estimated at upwards of 1,000, of which 80 were on the north side of the port, where the shoal water prevented any heavy vessel from getting within range, about 220 on the mole, about 95 on the eastern sea front, and most of the rest of the batteries on heights behind the town or in the environs. The guns were chiefly 32, 24 and 18-pounders, but there were also some heavier pieces and several enormous mortars. In addition, there were in port four 44-gun frigates, five large corvettes of from 24 to 30 guns and, perhaps, between 30 and 50 gun and mortar boats. The Moorish garrison consisted of at least 40,000 men. On their side, the attackers had 25 British and Dutch ships of approximately 946 guns of various sizes which fired 49,815 rounds of shot.[2a] The Dutch squadron was reported to have aided the British admirably.

Midshipman Elliot saw duty during the entire bombardment aboard the *Minden*, in which he had sailed from Plymouth; this 74-gun vessel fired 4,710 rounds of shot and suffered a loss of seven killed and 37 wounded.[2a] The *Minden*, with Exmouth's flagship the *Queen Charlotte*, and the *Impregnable*, *Albion* and *Superb*, were the five largest vessels and took up their front positions parallel with the external contour of the mole.

Exmouth humanely waved to the crowds on shore to indicate that he was about to fire, then the flagship opened, the other ships of the fleet joining in the fray as soon as their guns would bear. The fierce and sudden bombardment rapidly made its effects felt; everything exposed to the close fire of the ships tumbled into ruin. By 7 p.m., the town, arsenal, storehouses and vessels within the mole were burning briskly. Between 8 and 9 p.m., a British explosion vessel, the *Infernal*, was run on shore near the battery northward of the lighthouse and there blown up soon after 9 p.m.

The engagement continued until 10 p.m. when, ammunition threatening to give out and the hostile fire being nearly silenced, the ships by order began to cut their cables and springs and, after hauling and towing, to stand out before a light air which had just sprung up. By 2 a.m. of the 28th, the British-Dutch fleet had come to out of reach of the guns of Algiers, though still within the bright glare which was thrown far to seaward by the blaze

8

in the bay. Soon a violent thunderstorm burst upon both fleet and town. At daylight, Exmouth renewed his demands of the previous morning and, at the same time, began his preparations for recommencing bombardment. But the pirates had had enough. They quickly replied that the attackers' terms were acceptable. Conferences were held, and ultimately 1,083 Christian slaves were freed, a promise was given to abolish slave making, 382,500 dollars which had been paid by Naples and Sardinia by way of ransom were restored, an indemnity of 3,000 dollars, accompanied by a verbose apology and reinstatement, was tendered to the British Consul, and peace was made with the Netherlands. On 3rd September at midnight, Exmouth weighed to return home.

Numerical losses experienced by the British were 128 killed and 690 wounded; and by the Dutch 13 killed and 52 wounded. Estimates of the losses suffered by the Algerians put the number killed and wounded at from 4,000 to nearly 7,000.[2b]

It is impossible to believe that the fortifications, guns and gunners of Algiers in 1816 could have rivalled the European standard of the age. To have placed comparatively few heavy ships, as the Exmouth Expedition had, in close conflict with first-rate works, mounting several hundred guns, and manned by experienced gunners, would have been little short of madness. Had the Algerian defences been really as powerful as a paper summary of them suggests, a large force would have been sent to reduce them. But, certainly, the Algerians fought with great skill, action was exceptionally hot, and success gained was not easily won.

Yet success was brief for, within a few months of Exmouth's lesson to the Algerians, the Dey had begun to restore his fortresses, to recreate his navy, and to dispatch Tunisian pirates even into the North Sea, where they captured Hamburg vessels and were chased in vain by both the Dutch and the British.

But Charles Elliot did not see duty in these North Sea engagements, for, after the bombardment of Algiers, he was sent to the East Indies, where it had long been the unhappy chore of His Majesty's East Indian squadron to repress the ravages and punish the insolence of the pirates of the Persian Gulf.

Left to its own resources, the trade of India, as well as that tapping the wealth of the East Indies, early became an easy prey to the pirates which infested the coast of Malabar, where their principal rendezvous was the fort of Mulwhan to the southward of Bombay. The East India Company's marine could not contend against these sea-robbers of the Indies with any certainty of success for their attacks, either in ships of war or merchant vessels, were always conducted with spirit and skill, and the regular succession of calms during the fine weather monsoon afforded them every facility to manage their gunboats to the best advantage. These proas or undecked vessels of about 60 feet in length, carrying one 24-pound gun in the bow, preyed upon the company's cruisers and not infrequently the crews were put to death. So, since 1789 and the arrival of Commodore Cornwallis in India, it had been the duty of British ships of war to attempt to control the pirates to the eastward of the Cape of Good Hope. Within this broad span H.M.'s ships met pirates from the Gulf of Persia as well as those from the straits of Malacca.[1a] Moreover, it was the duty of the East Indies fleet to control attacks from French privateers who based chiefly on the islands of France and Bourbon. The shelter afforded to shipping, and the resources possessed by the first of these islands for equipping and victualling both ships of war and privateers, long had enabled the enterprising French to cause incalculable injury to Britain's Indian commerce.[1b]

This lucrative trade to the Far East was the result of the vast toil of many a generation of the English, and the Home Government constantly was bombarded with protests bewailing the lack of aid to the tall-masted British frigates which, so long and so bravely, had sailed the robber-infested waters of the East. In 1809, Captain John Wainwright had commanded a detachment of sloops-of-war which thoroughly chastised these marauders.[1c] But, after a lapse of nine years, again they began to follow their former practices and the government at Bombay fitted out a land expedition to co-operate with His Majesty's East Indian Navy to try to destroy, once and for all, by land and sea, all of England's piratical enemies in the Eastern Seas.[1d]

In this piratical repression, Elliot served, until the year 1820, under the flag of Sir Richard King, who for many years had held the chief command on the East Indian station.[3b] The year 1819-20 proved a bright one for the East Indian fleet, for then expeditions against the pirates of Ras-al-Khyma, in the Persian Gulf, were undertaken, and in these operations the piratical works in that area were taken and destroyed and all vessels in port were burnt or sunk.

From the East Indies, Elliot was assigned and transferred to several flags engaged in the defences of the West African coast where, as had been suspected at the time in England, the lesson given in 1816 to the Dey of Algiers had not been sufficiently severe to be lasting. The Moorish pirates had continued to commit outrages on the high seas and to violate the sanctity of the British Consulate.[2c]

Midshipman Elliot, in the early 1820's, years to him fleeting but precious, successively joined several commands before attaining officer rank. In 1820-21, he joined the *Starling* (10) cutter, then on Home station service and under Lieutenant-Commander John Reeve.[3c,g] Next, for the young seaman came assignment to the *Queen Charlotte* (100), flagship at Portsmouth of Sir James Hawkins Whitshed, at the time renowned for Napoleonic boat affairs and later to become Admiral of the Fleet.[3d] In June 1821, Sir Robert Mends, also a naval hero of England's recent wars with France, hoisted a broad pennant in the *Iphigenia* (42) as Commodore of the squadron employed on the western coast of Africa, and there Mister Elliot served.[3e] After a few months on the *Iphigenia*, he went to the *Myrmidon* (20), under Captain Henry John Leeke,[3f] and that vessel soon experienced a bit of action in saving a Portuguese schooner from being wrecked in the Sierra Leone River. On a subsequent occasion, Leek carried the *Myrmidon* over the fearful bar of the river Bonny for the purpose of attacking two slave vessels which had beaten off British boats and wounded two officers and several men. In this skirmish, after the capture of the slavers had been accomplished, the *Myrmidon* tied up to the coast and compelled the native king of that part of West Africa to enter into a treaty fixing the duty to be paid by British merchants trading to the river for palm oil—an arrangement which in particular answered a long cry of the importers of Liverpool.

Charles Elliot attained the rank of Lieutenant on 11th June 1822[3g] while in the *Myrmidon* and, on 19th June, again was appointed, in that new capacity, to the *Iphigenia*, Commodore Robert Mends' flagship, engaged on the western coast of Africa.[3g,h] On 22nd March 1823, Lieutenant Elliot joined the *Hussar* (46), Captain George Harris, then fitting for the Jamaica station. Weeks later,[3g] the *Hussar* put into the Caribbean, waters alive with slave traders, where the next several years were to pass quickly and profitably for Elliot. On 19th June and 30th August 1825, he was appointed to the command there of the *Union* and *Renegade* schooners;[3g] and, on 1st January 1826, we find him nominated Acting-Commander of the *Seraphis*, convalescent-ship, lying at Port Royal, centre of Jamaica's flourishing slave trade. On 14th April following, he was confirmed into the *Magnificent*, hospital and store ship, then achored at Port Royal.[3g] After a further employment in the *Bustard* (10) and *Harlequin* (18), on the same Jamaica station, Charles Elliot was promoted, by commission dated 28th August 1828,[3g] to the rank of Captain and placed on half pay.

Thus had Elliot spent fourteen very formative years on active duty with the Royal Navy. While protecting the British Dominions in home waters and in the waters of the Old World and the New, he became nurtured not only in the lessons of the sea but buttressed with first-hand knowledge and experience of the far-flung locales along the ocean roads where, later, he was to participate in empire-building.

BIBLIOGRAPHY & REFERENCES

1 Brenton, Edward Pelham, *The Naval History of Great Britain from the year MDCCLXXXIII to MDCCCXXII*, Vol. I. London: C. Rice, 1825.
  a pp.334-37; *b* p.396; *c* pp.394-401; *d* pp.265-67.
2 Clowes, William Laird, *The Royal Navy—A History from the Earlest Times to the Present*, Vol. VI. London: Sampson, Low, Marston and Co., 1901.
  a p.227; *b* pp.227-30; *c* pp.235-37.
3 O'Byrne's *Naval Biographical Dictionary*.
  a p.125; *b* p.613; *c* p.963; *d* p.1286; *e* p.754; *f* p.644; *g* p.332; *h* p.754.

III

The Protector of Slaves
Slavery in British Guiana

ON 2nd February, 1830, Captain Charles Elliot was 'appointed by letter from the Secretary of State at the annual Salary in Sterling of £1,017, 14s.' as 'Protector of Slaves to British Guiana.'[6] From 28th August 1828, when he was advanced to post rank, Elliot virtually retired from the navy, being actively and almost continuously employed in the services of the Colonial or Foreign Offices.[20a, 21a]

The internal history of the three Guiana colonies long was concerned mainly with the question of the supply of labour to work the sugar, cotton, and coffee plantations, whose prosperity depended on negro labour and whose prosperity was considerably checked after 1807 by the abolition of the slave trade.[14a] The stress of the Napoleonic wars quelled, for a time, the pleas of missionary enterprise for amelioration of the condition of the West Indian slaves, then British humanitarianism again began to assert itself.[7a]

Elliot came to his new appointment some 200 years after Sir Walter Raleigh's adventures at the mouths of the 'bevvtiful empyre's' trio of great rivers, the Berbice, Demerara, and Essequibo, and his coastal explorations of Trinidad and his voyage up the Orinoco.[16] Though discovered earlier by Spanish explorers in 1499-1500, Guiana was uncolonized until 1580, and, then, by the pioneering and enterprising Netherlanders who, seeing in this part of the Spanish Main a land not unlike their dyked motherland, revelled in their efforts.[15a] Raleigh prophesied in his *The Discoverie of Gviana* that whatever prince should possess his El Dorado—'Lands of the Inner Sea,'—should be lord of more gold, and of a more beautiful empire, and of more cities and people, than either the King of Spain or the Great Turk.[16a] Unsuccessful attempts to follow the Dutch example were made by Raleigh and other British adventurers but the year was 1663 before the settlement of an English colony was effected under Lord Willoughby.[15]

From time to time, the country knew several sovereignties, Spanish, Dutch, English, and, also, French and, then, in 1802, it was restored to the Dutch. In 1803, England retook Guiana which, in 1814, finally was ceded by treaty.[14b, 17, 18] Among the records that came into the possession of Great Britain when the final territorial transfer was made were the reports sent home by the higher officials of the Dutch West India Company and, upon reading the reports penned by one Laurens Storm Van's Gravesande, writing from Guiana for a period of 34 years, from 1738 to 1772, the Government was reminded of Raleigh's 16th-century accounts and singular prophecy.[10a] Interest was rekindled in the country which, when the three colonies of Berbice, Demerara, and Essequibo were united in 1831 as the crown colony of British Guiana, was to become Britain's sole possession on the South American mainland.

Sir Benjamin D'Urban, accused of a bias in favour of the planters in the West Indies when he served as Governor of the Leeward Islands, 1820-1824, became Governor of Demerara and Essequibo from 26th April 1824 and, on 21st July 1831, became Governor of United British Guiana, which office he was to hold until 1833, when Elliot was called home from Guiana.[8a] On 7th September 1825, D'Urban, after much opposition from the Guiana planters, proved to be a man who saw a side of the slave question that the owners desired unseen. Together with the Guiana Court of Policy, on that fateful day, Governor D'Urban passed an ordinance entitled 'An Ordinance for the Religious Instructions of Slaves and for Meliorating their Condition.' The Ordinance was published on 15th October and was to go into effect on 1st January 1826.[12a] Provision was made for the appointment of a 'Protector of Slaves',[12a] a title conveying a satire upon the conduct of the community, and certainly not very complimentary to the Governor himself.

The duties of this officer, the Protector of Slaves, were vexatious and arduous. His position was likely to render him obnoxious to many of the colonists, while it required great prudence, judgment, and firmness to enable him to deal with possibly untrue complaints of the slaves on the one side and to soothe the offended dignity of owners and employers on the other. The slaves were secured an immunity from labour (except in certain specific cases) from sunset on Saturday to sunrise on Monday; field work was limited from 6 a.m. to 6 p.m., with two hours intermission; the Act prohibited the whip from being carried into the field, abolished the whipping of women, limited punishment to 25 lashes, required a record of punishments to be kept, secured to the slaves the privileges of marriage, of acquiring and holding property, and of purchasing their freedom. An officer from England, Colonel A. W. Young, was appointed to the new office [12a] and, from Young's proclamations and ordinances, 1826-30, the nature of Elliot's career in Guiana can be surmised.

Protectors of Slaves and Assistant Protectors were not to own or manage slaves, and were to be warranted in entering into negro houses on estates; privilege was given to slaves to pass and repass to Protectors to make complaints; Protectors could summon and examine witnesses and witnesses not attending might be committed to gaol; the Protector was not to act as magistrate but could act as coroner and, also, could appear in behalf of slaves prosecuted; Protectors were to prohibit Sunday traffic, under penalties; and, with certain exceptions, were to determine regulations about use of the whip and forfeitures of slaves in cases of cruelty and ill-treatment; slaves were made competent to marry and to apply for such license to the Protector; slaves were not to be proprietors of boats, ammunition, etc.; 'relationships of slaves were to be attended to'; fees of office and duties of manumissions were abolished; slaves might effect the purchase of their freedom by a compulsory process; evidence of slaves was to be admitted. The Act, as interpreted and appended by the first Protector, came to include rules and regulations respecting the food and maintenance of slaves, the duration of various labours, clothing, medical attendance, religious worship, and other important subjects.[1a]

On 2nd February, 1830, 'An Order of His Majesty in Council for Improving the Condition of the Slaves' was issued, 'Regular Reports from Protectors' were required, and it was as a result of this that Elliot was sent out.[4a] The Reports were to include a definite schedule of contents:

Offences committed.	Evidence.
Absence of punishment.	Defence.
Defaulters.	Result of proceedings.
Name, age, sex, etc. of complainant.	Explanatory remarks.
	Employment of slaves on Sunday.
Name of owner.	Marriages and separations.
Substance of complaint and proceedings thereupon.	Voluntary and compulsory manumissions.[5a]

Upon arrival at cholera-ridden Georgetown,[III] Elliot encountered much local agitation to have colony officials paid out 'of one Chest, that of the Colony under the Colonial Receiver', instead of 'the outmoded King's Chest',[4b] which had been 'originated in Dutch time' [4c] and which, by 1830, was considered far too 'moderate'.[4c] For the three years he was Protector,

III Georgetown, at the mouth of the Demerara, was founded by the British in 1781 and made the seat of government of the combined colonies of Essequibo and Demerara, 1784; formerly called Stabroek during Dutch occupation, it was renamed Georgetown in 1812.

Elliot was paid probably £500 annually.[4d] The Court of Policy held that

> As to the Salaries of the two Assistant Protectors of Slaves, these were refused on the ground that there appeared no necessity for the further creation of such offices, beyond what already exists, as the duties belonging to them can be performed by resident Proprietors and other respectable Inhabitants without emolument.[4e]

For the year 1831-32, Elliot, in addition to his work as Protector of Slaves, served as a member of the Court of Policy. This body dealt with such of the colony's problems as the maintenance of the Colony House. Mrs Elizabeth Embleton, 'Colony House Keeper,' had died and the

> . . . Executor (Coxall) not having received payment from the Colony for his disbursements in keeping up that Establishment during the present year (1831-32) at length found himself without the means of providing those indispensable necessaries of daily consumption required by the few Country Members of this Court who while in attendance on their Public Duty, lived at the Colony House.[4f]

The Colonial Receiver was authorized by the Court of Policy to issue to Coxall 'a Sum of Two Thousand two hundred guilders on account of his claim sent in against the Colony.'[4g] Other concerns of Elliot's term on the Court of Policy were the 'Establishment of Board of Health in the respective District of Demerary and Essequebo and of Berbice';[4h,i] and the repeal of an ordinance (previously passed by the Court of Policy) 'to establish and constitute Inferior Courts of Civil Justice in British Guiana';[4g] and, proportionment of the moieties of the salaries of the Governor, the Chief Justice, the Second Puisne Judge, and the Protector of Slaves between the King's Chests of Berbice, Demerara, and Essequibo.[4j] Furthermore, the Court of Policy was concerned because

> The Colony which has at a heavy expense provided Churches for every Parish and good Clergymen for the same, are now prevented from raising Taxes for their payment, and also from raising sums of money for the support of the poor at a time of great distress, and when the people are under the necessity of providing against the Cholera, by erecting of Hospitals without a shilling to pay for them, *merely* because the Governor's Instructions *forbid him to allow the Legislature to raise the Taxes.*[4b]

As Protector of Slaves, Elliot's initial concern was a population census. These tabulations, for the year 1831, he recorded as follows:[1b]

			Males	Females
Whites	...	...	419	104
Free Blacks	...	...	454	707
Slaves	...	...	10,897	9,281
Total	...	...	55,494	47,044

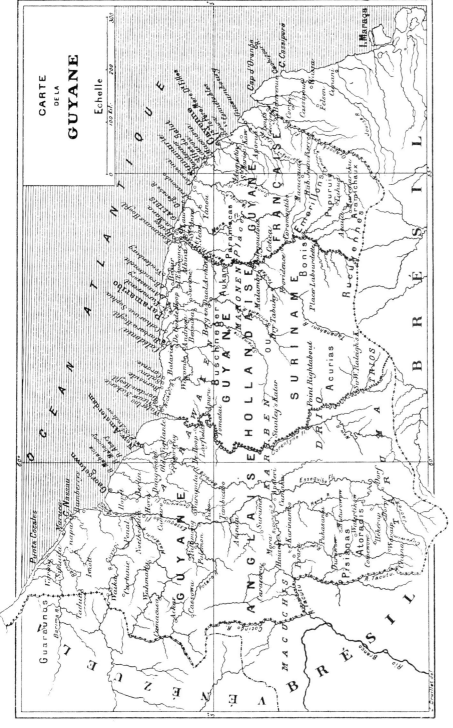

Carte de la Guyane (Tripot, J., *La Guyane*. Paris: Plon Nourrit et Cie, 1910)

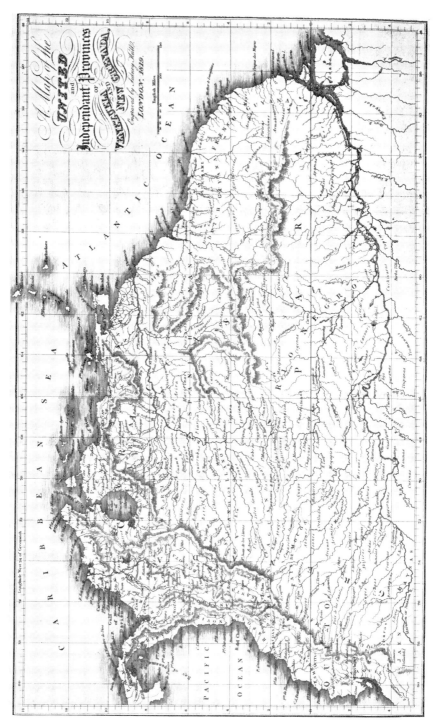

Map of the United and Independent Provinces of Venezuela and New Grenada (Dauxion-Lavaysse, Jean François, *A Statistical, Commercial and Political Description of Venezuela, Trinidad, Margarita and Tobago*. London: W. Shackell, Printer, 1820)

To acquaint the Colonial Office with the conditions of slaves in the colony, Elliot dispatched to London several detailed reports. Types of offences reported were:

attempting to poison
attempting to ravish
attempting to murder
attempting to commit suicide
cutting others with cutlasses
incendiaries
killing and destroying stock
cruelty to animals
housebreaking and stealing
theft, petty larceny
stock stealing
receiving stolen goods

striking manager or driver
biting overseer
holding and tearing driver's shirt
insolence
insubordination
abusive language to owners
absconding from work
quarrelling
maltreating children
infidelity among slaves
father selling daughter to
    prostitution

(average from 1 ravish to 127 theft, petty larceny).[3a]

Additional types of offences committed were:

refusing to work
neglecting person
introducing rum on estate
bad work
fake complaints

harbouring runaway
carelessness with fire
illtreating wives
selling working utensils
drunkenness [3b]

To this portion of his report Elliot appended the note that, as Protector, he was constantly being pressed by owners 'to employ their slaves on Sunday in works of necessity' and that, just as constantly, he replied that 'the Protector has not received any notice respecting Sunday work'.[3c] Nor is evidence found that the Protector asked the Home Office for any such notice.

Elliot, reporting his examination of the Punishment Record Books which the planters were required to keep, noted the type and severity of punishment: stripes (average punishment being 55 stripes),[3b] stocks (1-3 days),[3b] flogging,[3d] and placing in the dark-room.[3e] The slaves themselves, their Protector informed London, complained of 'beating with a rope without cause';[3f] suffering punishment because, as relatives, they took victuals to hospitalized slaves;[3g] being forced to labour while ill;[3h] tasks assigned were too heavy;[3i] the quantity of work required was impossible;[3j] 'not being allowed to work late one day so as to finish early the next';[3k] 'inability to identify the specified type of tree (usually Bullettree) to fell and being flogged'.[3l,m]

B
17

On 10th July 1831, Downing Street was 'concerned with much regret that very little or no diminution has taken place in the punishments inflicted by the domestic authority of the owner'.[3n] That same week, on 16th July, Elliot's Report to the Foreign Office estimated that 'it appears that 4,582 Punishments have been inflicted on a Slave population of 18,220 persons in little more than four months, being as nearly as possible in the proportion of one in four'.[3o] Horrified, Elliot cited the example 'that from Plantation Ubile et Paisible, Manager Mr Corbett, which exhibits the extraordinary number of 420 punishments inflicted on 145 slaves in little more than four months, being very nearly three times as many punishments as there were slaves on the Estate'.[3o] Concluding his Report on this particular plantation, Elliot wrote: '. . . of punishments inflicted I have found none which can at all compare with that from Plantation Ubile et Paisible. It is difficult to conceive any circumstances which could justify such severity . . .' [3o] 'Slaves Walter and Vincent complained that they had not enough to eat and they exhibited a small calabash with ground Indian corn, which they state was their allowance for three days.' [3p] Elliot 'strongly suspected the slaves on that Estate (Ubile et Paisible) were forming a combination against the Manager'.[3q]

Elliot's Report was forwarded to Governor Sir B. D'Urban who forwarded it to London, apparently on 18th December 1831.[3r] Downing Street's reply, addressed to 'The Protector of Slaves, British Guiana', was dated 21st April 1832, and signed by one, Goderich, who wrote:

> I have observed with much regret the very large number of punishments inflicted upon Slaves during the period comprised in this Report amounting to no less than 5,307 on 18,911 Slaves.[3s]

The Protector's Report for the period January to June 1832 recorded:[3t]

Total number of slaves comprised in Report	...	...	17,482
Total number of punishments inflicted	...	...	3,720
Total number of males punished	...	...	2,214
Total number of females punished	...	...	1,506

In a private letter to his friend Lord Howick, then Under-Secretary for the Colonies, Captain Elliot, early in 1832, with a bitter pen, wrote:

> As to my office it is a delusion. There is no protection for the Slave Population; and they will very shortly take the matter into their own hands, and destroy the Property. The only way of saving these Countries is to give the Slaves a reasonable share in the produce of their Labour.
>
> I am desperately unpopular, although I am sure I have not intended to do my duty captiously. But the fact is that this Colony is in a state of rebellion; the administration of Justice obstructed or totally defeated—no taxes paid—the most

vehement clamour, not only against the Laws themselves, but against the Law-making power. What remedy for all these evils is sent out to us? Despatches full of hopes and exhortations, of advice to repent and behave better. This impunity gives strength to the growth of the Evil. The Order in Council is a dead letter and a dead letter contemned and decried in the most insulting terms. But if it were respected, would the Slave have benefited to such an Extent as he ought to be benefited, *and as he looks to be benefited?* No such thing. Setting aside the improbability of ensuring the observation of such a body of Law, I do deeply feel its inadequacy to present circumstances. You have brought forward the Slave to a certain point of civilization and intelligence, and he perceives the utter insufficiency of your System either for his further advancement or for his controul. What should be given to the Slaves is *such a state of Freedom as they are now fit for.*[8b]

Elliot's final Protector's Report,[3u] dated November 1833, recorded:[3v]

Total number of slaves comprised in Report	17,620
Total number of punishments inflicted	4,748
Total number of males punished	2,858
Total number of females punished	1,890

Frequently, the Public Record Office inserts the words, 'Folios number —and—are blank and have not been copied,' across the blank pages of the lengthy Reports required of the Protector. Equally frequent did Elliot close his various extracts from Record Books, Hospital Books, Protector's Reports, Complaints, and Case Records with the comment: 'The Owners want courts, not Protector, to decide.'

Meanwhile, and for 30 years past, since 1807 and the abolition of the commerce in slaves, emancipation had been the dream of the abolitionists and such reports and letters home as Elliot despatched during the several years he served as Protector of Slaves in British Guiana served to enhance the already-present religious fervour of the cause. Throughout the latter part of 1832, discussions proceeded between Elliot's friend, Lord Howick, the anti-slave Under-Secretary for the Colonies, and such Government men as James Stephen and Henry Taylor, on the means of abolishing slavery. And, by 1832, the Imperial Government itself slowly came to realize that its policy and the power of public opinion must by their very momentum bring abolition very soon. The Great Debate which was to lead to victory for the old Anti-Slavery Society of Wilberforce—the emancipation of slaves throughout the Empire—was in the making. Early in December 1832, a memorandum by Howick was circulated among members of the Cabinet, urging that an Abolition Bill should be brought in during the coming session. With some modifications of form rather than of substance, Lord Howick's plan was considered by a Cabinet

Committee consisting of Lords Althorp, Goderich, and Holland, Lord John Russell, the Duke of Richmond, and Sir James Graham. With some hesitation, the plan was approved and then met strong opposition from the leading West Indians in England.[8c,d] Sir John Francis Davis, long prominent because of his connections with China and with the East India Company, highly commended to the Government his friend, Captain Charles Elliot, reporting that, in his opinion, 'the talents, information, and temper of that gentleman (Elliot) would render him eminently suited to the chief station in this country (China)' and, furthermore, Davis noted and called to the Government's attention his belief that Elliot was serving with distinction under the Colonial Office as Protector of Slaves and a member of the Government in British Guiana.[11a] Consequently, in 1833, Elliot was ordered home to put his knowledge at the disposal of the Imperial Government at the time when the great measure for the abolition of slavery was being prepared.[3w] For his helpful service he won the approval of the Secretary of State, Lord Stanley, the Lord Chancellor, Sir Robert Peel, and others.[11a] Lord Stanley, after many conferences with Elliot concerning the former Protector's first-hand information as to slavery in the West Indies, introduced and, with great difficulty and many modifications, carried a very different plan which provided for substantial compensation to the planters and for a six years' apprenticeship—the old idea of a gradual transition from slavery to freedom in an altered form.[8c]

On his return home, Elliot's friendship with Sir John Francis Davis led to his taking up a new post in China.

BIBLIOGRAPHY & REFERENCES

MICROFILM

1 *British Guiana, Blue Books of Statistics.* C.O.R. 116/145 and 152-202.
116/178: *a* p.72; *Description of Office of Protector of Slaves to British Guiana.*
116/178: *b* p.114.
2 *British Guiana, Despatches from Downing Street,* 1828–34. C.O.R. 116/146-51.
3 *British Guiana, Reports of Protectors of Slaves,* 1828–34. C.O.R. 116/146-202.
116/146: *a* p.108; *f* p.160; *g* p.163; *h* p.166; *i* p.170; *j* p.171; *k* p.173; *l* p.177; *n* p.1; *o* p.2; *p* p.3; *q* p.5.
116/148: *b* p.85; *d* p.202; *m* pp.340-95; *r* pp.15-28; *s* pp.3-14.
116/149: *e* p.159.
116/150: *t* pp.1-8.
116/151: *c* p.250.
116/152: *u* pp.1-60; *v* p.8.
116/153: *w* p.126.
4 *British Guiana, Sessional Papers.* C.O.R. 114/12-13; 116/145-202.
116/146: *a* p.1ff.
114/12: *b* p.409; *c* p.408; *d* p.419; *e* p.389; *f* p.373; *g* p.377; *h* p.375; *i* pp.372-79; *j* p.384.
5 *British Guiana, New (1830) Law Reports.* C.O.R. 116/146.
a pp.20-22 and ff.

PRINTED

6 *Public Record Office Lists and Indexes, No. XXXVI List of Colonial Office Records Preserved in the Public Record Office.* London: His Majesty's Stationery Office, 1911. Permission to microfilm granted by The Cleveland Public Library.

7 Abel, Annie Heloise, and Klingberg, Frank J. (eds.), *A Sidelight on Anglo-American Relations, 1839– 1858, Furnished by the Correspondence of Lewis Tappan and Others with the British and Foreign Anti- Slavery Society.* Lancaster, Pennsylvania: The Association for the Study of Negro Life and History Incorporated, 1927.
a p.1ff.

8 Bell, Kenneth N., and Morrell, W. P. (eds.), *Select Documents on British Colonial Policy, 1830–1860.* Oxford: The Clarendon Press, 1928.
a p.566; *b* p.382; *c* p.370ff; *d* p.383ff.

9 Donnan, Elizabeth, *Documents Illustrative of the Slave Trade to America,* Vol. I. Washington: Carnegie Institution, 1930–35. (This gives a useful resume of the early slave trade.)

10 Harris, C. A., and de Villiers, J. A. J. (compilers), *Extracts from the Despatches written by Lauren Storm Van's Gravesande to the Directors of the Zeeland Chamber of the West India Company,* Vol. I. London: The Hakluyt Society, 1911.
a pp.1-8.

11 Costin, W. C., *Great Britain and China, 1833–1860.* Oxford: The Clarendon Press, 1937.
a p.31.

12 Dalton, Henry G., *The History of British Guiana,* Vol. I. London: Longman, Brown, Green, and Longmans, 1855.
a p.364.

13 Dauxion-Lavaysse, Jean François, *A Statistical, Commercial, and Political Description of Venezuela, Trinidad, Margarita, and Tobago, containing various Anecdotes and Observations, Illustrative of the Past and Present State of These Interesting Countries.* London: W. Shackell, Printer, 1820.

14 Edmundson, The Rev. G. C., *The Relations of Great Britain with Guiana,* from *Transactions of the Royal Historical Society,* Vol. I. London: Offices of the Society, 1923.
a pp.1-17; *b* pp.1-8.

15 Pascoe, C. F., *Two Hundred Years of the S.P.G.: An Historical Account of the Society for the Propagation of the Gospel in Foreign Parts, 1701–1900.* (Based on a Digest of the Society's Records.) London: Published at the Society's Office, 1901.
a p.242.

16 Ralegh, Sir Walter, *The Discoverie of Gviana.* London, 1596. Reprint: Cassell and Company, Limited, London, Paris, New York and Melbourne, 1887. The University of Texas Rare Books Collection.
a p.23.

17 Roberts, W. Adolphe, *Lands of the Inner Sea.* New York: Coward-McCann, Inc., 1948.

18 Rodway, James, *Guiana: British, Dutch, and French.* London and Leipsic: T. Fisher Unwin, MCMXII. (Gives the early history of Guiana, from the aborigines and pioneer settlements through the Dutch, French and British eras.)

19 Tripot, J., *La Guyane.* Paris: Plon-Nourrit et Cie., 1910.

20 O'Byrne's *Naval Biographical Dictionary.*
a p. 332.

21 Leslie Stephen, *Dictionary of National Biography,* Vol. XVII. 62 vols. London: Smith, Elder and Company, 1889–Present.
a p. 251.

IV

The Summit of a Career
Far Eastern Trade and the Opium War

━━━━━━━⟨≈≈≈⟩━━━━━━━

WESTERN trade with China had followed discovery of the great waterways to the East at the end of the fifteenth century and, during the next four centuries, it had been hedged in by a burdensome system of restrictions and regulations, all tending to emphasize the social and political superiority of the Chinese.[IV, 18a]

In 1684, the Emperor granted the right to the East India Company to establish a factory at Canton. In 1795, another Emperor refused to do anything more for the Macartney mission. Then, Europe survived the Napoleonic Wars and from them England emerged the most powerful nation in the world. To the diplomats of Trafalgar and Waterloo it appeared unbelievable that the Court at Peking should continue the ceremony and thought of by-gone centuries. So, in 1816, the Amherst mission went out to China, and accomplished nothing. Meanwhile, the British merchants at Canton struggled on in a situation unameliorated for two centuries. But, around 1800, where the diplomats and envoys had failed the merchants of the East India Company were to hit upon a means of forcing upon China the British Government's conventional international procedures in commerce and diplomacy. About 1800, the British offered a new commodity, opium, called 'foreign mud' in international discourse, and the profitable increase in its importation into China corresponds with the British occupation of India and the golden days of the British East India Company. In 1833, the Foreign Office assumed responsibility for the China Trade, following the abolition of the East India Company's monopoly, inheriting, among other things, the opium problem.

IV For a discussion of Confucian philosophy as an economic force confronted by Western traders, the expiration of the Charter of the East India Company, Free Trade, the Napier and Elliot Missions, opium smuggling, and the exertions of the native government for suppression.

The poppy had been known in China for twelve centuries, and its medicinal use for nine centuries. About the middle of the seventeenth century, the practice of mixing opium with tobacco for smoking purposes was introduced into China. The habit was indulged in by the Dutch in Java, was taken by them to Formosa, whence it spread to Amoy and the mainland. Perhaps by the close of the eighteenth century, opium was first smoked by itself. At the beginning of the eighteenth century, foreign opium was introduced by the Portuguese from Goa; by 1729, the Emperor Yung Ching was alarmed and issued the first anti-opium edict. Severe penalties, both on the sale of opium and on the opening of opium-smoking divans, were enacted. However, the lucrative importation continued and, by 1790, it amounted to over 4,000 chests annually.[v] In 1796, opium smoking again was prohibited and, in 1800, the importation of foreign opium was declared illegal. Now, opium was contraband; yet imports continued to grow.[vi]

Since December 1833, Elliot had been serving on the Napier Commission to China, Napier being appointed Superintendent of the Trade of British Subjects in China by the British Government. As Master Attendant, Elliot had charge of all British ships and crews within the Bocca Tigris, or 'The Bogue', the narrow channel between the upper and lower Pearl rivers between Canton and Hong Kong; the lower river constitutes the bay twenty miles wide between Hong Kong and Macao; below Canton the upper Pearl is joined by the Tung from the east. In January 1835, Elliot was appointed Third Superintendent, and in December 1836 was recommended for the post of Senior Superintendent. Elliot was the choice of Davis (who followed Napier as Superintendent) for his successor and Davis had reported to the Home Government his own high opinion of Elliot's talents, information, and temper as eminently suiting Elliot to the chief station in China. Palmerston, British Foreign Minister, recalled that, even before the appointment to the minor office of Master Attendant in Lord Napier's Commission, Elliot had served Britain with distinction, not only in the Royal Navy but under the Colonial Office as Protector of Slaves and a member of the Government in British Guiana. Moreover, in 1833, he had been ordered home in order that his knowledge might be

---

v A chest contained from 1 picul, 133-1/3 lb., to 150 lb., and the price at Canton fluctuated between $5,000 and $1,000 per chest.

vi Hosea Ballou Morse, *The International Relations of the Chinese Empire*, gives these figures:

1800	.	2,000 chests disposed of in China
1821–28	.	9,708 chests disposed of in China
1828–35	.	18,712 chests disposed of in China
1835–39	.	30,000 chests disposed of in China

See Morse's *Opium Tables and Notes*, I, 209-11, for detailed figures for the periods 1800-21 and 1821-39.

put before the Imperial Government in the days when the great measure for the abolition of slavery throughout the Empire was being prepared. Even Sir Robert Peel, the Secretary of State, the Lord Chancellor, and others, had expressed their indebtedness to the young Elliot for his helpful advice. And Palmerston realised that Elliot himself desired a position of authority and responsibility in the East. During 1836, Elliot's energies were devoted to establishing and regularizing commercial relations with Japan —a policy denounced by the *Quarterly Review*[26a] in July of that year and ignored, until October 1838, by the Whig organ, the *Edinburgh Review*.[20a]

Moreover, Elliot was already known to Palmerston through his private correspondence with Lennox Conyngham of the Foreign Office. He had been writing of 'the heedless spirit in active operation at Canton' and to the effect that King George's conciliatory policy was not generally approved by the British merchants in Canton. Furthermore, Napier, Davis, and Robinson (Davis' successor) had not taken up the cautious and conciliatory instructions with the spirit necessary to give them effect. Elliot wrote his friend that he hoped the Government would express its determination to discountenance the temper shown by the majority of the merchants (the belligerent home merchants) and that, personally, he was convinced that the British Superintendent's stress upon the point of direct official intercourse with the Viceroy, without the intervention of the Hong merchants, was not warranted by their instructions and had only served to delay communications. Also, Elliot deprecated sending to China anyone with high official rank, until the Chinese asked for such a man; as in 1614, Sir Thomas Roe had warned the Company that an ambassador was not honoured in the Celestial Empire; and, like Roe more than two centuries before, Elliot did not advocate the actual annexation of Chinese territory, due partly to the factor of expense to the Home Government and partly from doubt whether present commercial and financial advantages would continue. The value of a commercial treaty was minimized by Elliot, who said he feared the English would suffer from their inadequate knowledge of the Chinese language while the Chinese, by faithless and perplexing construction of terms, would not only irritate but injure the English. The business of disturbing that most prosperous commerce, smuggling, was viewed by Elliot as too risky: he felt that those few merchants who thought it scandalous that the Emperor should be defrauded and that they, the merchants, should have to resort to smuggling, only wanted to attempt the social, commercial, political, and religious regeneration of the Chinese Empire. Caution, conciliation, and attention to improve opportunities were Elliot's suggestions by which His Majesty's officers in China might win the confidence of the Chinese Government. A means of repressing rashness upon the part of the King's subjects was an urgent need, for then, and only then, would the provincial authorities be convinced of the British Government's good will. The instructions that had been given to the commissioners were good ones, thought Elliot, though, like Robinson, he felt that remodelling and reduction would improve the establishment.

On 14th December 1836, Elliot, upon receiving his appointment despatch from Palmerston, signed as Senior Superintendent of the Trade of British Subjects in China and wrote London:

> In conformity with these instructions I have this day assumed the Chief placing in the Commission. And with the expression of my thanks to Your Lordship I beg to convey my assurance, that I shall endeavour to justify the appointment by a steady determination faithfully to discharge the duties intrusted to me. I apply myself to that purpose with a strong persuasion that a conciliatory disposition to respect the usages, and above all to refrain from shocking the prejudices of this Government is the course at once most consonant with the magnanimity of the British Nation and with the Substantial interests at stake in the maintenance of peaceful commercial relations with this Empire. . . . I do not propose to protract the actual interruption of our public communications upon the ground that we have a right to a direct official communication with the Vice Roy. . . . I am not blind to the inconvenience of a channel of communication through the Hong Merchants, but in my judgment the mischief of a continued adherence, to their suspension of all responsible intercourse with the Authorities is incalculably greater.[1a]

Immediately upon becoming Chief Superintendent, 14th December, 1836,[1a] Elliot endeavoured to open communications with the Provincial authorities and perceived that the arrival of Palmerston's despatch (appointment orders) afforded him a favourable pretext for addressing himself to the Viceroy, the Governor of the Two Provinces.[1b] On 22nd December, the Viceroy replied, apparently in truly Chinese essence, criticizing the Chief Superintendent's title and ordering him to remain at Macao until the Emperor's wishes were known. On 28th December, Captain Elliot replied to the haughty Viceroy acquiescing in the order; but to his Home Government he wrote, signing as Chief Superintendent:

> No. 8—despatch No. 4. Macao 28th December 1836
>
> In the conversation I had with the Hong merchants this morning I took occasion to explain to them very fully all points connected with my arrival, and the nature of my public occupations since I have resided here.
>
> If my name has been improperly reported it must be owing to some mistake of the Pilots.
>
> My Commission of Authority is signed by my Gracious Sovereign, but my

25

despatches lately received as to the performance of my duties are signed by His Majesty's Minister.

My duty at Canton will be to conduct the public business of my Nation and by all possible means to preserve the Peace which so happily subsists between the two countries.

Charles Elliot.
Senior Superintendent.[1c]

Then, two days later, on 30th December, he informed Downing Street of his first diplomatic brush with the Celestial authorities and explained to Palmerston:

> ... Another reason too had suggested itself to me in recommendation of this prompt application to the Governor (besides the reason that delay in the communication of his appointment might be construed in a very suspicious nature): It seemed that a communication forwarded on the very recent receipt of Instructions from His Majesty's Government would of itself be a state of circumstances, well calculated to induce weighty motives disposing the Governor to lend a reasonable attention to moderate and unsuspicious overtures, respectfully submitted for his Excellency's adoption.
>
> The translation of this paper was sealed up and directed in the same form as the Select Committee of Super Cargoes had been accustomed to superscribe Documents to the Governor's address. In other words the superscription bore the Chinese character (稟 Pin) carrying in our language the signification of 'an address from an Inferior to a Superior'—It was then placed in an open envelope to the address of the Senior Hong Merchant, and the whole Inclosure was transmitted with the accompanying confidential letter to the Agents of the East India Company at Canton, and to two members of the Principal British Firms at that place.[1d]

Elliot, in this same letter to Palmerston, wrote that, from his experience and association with the Chinese, he was of the opinion that it would be wise for England, in the consideration of Chinese Official Papers, to aim at 'the detection of their real spirit' and that it would be 'a sounder course steadily to look at the material of these instruments, and to draw our conclusions from these, rather than from the manner in which it is the custom of these people to dress or cover up their purposes'.[1e]

Several months later, the Chinese authorities got around to Elliot's request to enter Canton. Downing, in his *Stranger in China*, records that the Viceroy of Quantung sent a 'Memorial' to his Imperial Majesty telling of Elliot's wish to reside in the Provincial City.[18b] The object of Elliot's residence there, as well as the attitude of the native government towards not only Elliot himself but all the English traders as well, cannot be better illustrated, perhaps, than by the Viceroy's 'Memorial' which informed the Emperor that

'Farther, of all the foreign barbarian merchants who have been allowed to frequent the port of Canton, the English have had the greatest trade. Hitherto they have had a Company, and their trade has been controlled by four principal merchants (1st, 2nd, 3rd, and 4th, taepans). Their ships arrived during the seventh and eighth months annually; and, having finished their barter, left the port within the first and second months of the following year; after which the taepans requested a passport, and went to Macao, where they remained until the seventh month, when they again requested a passport, and proceeded to the Provincial City to transact their business: such have been the regulations.

Upon the dissolution of the Company's factory, the taepans ceased to come hither, and its affairs were placed under the management of other men; and Governor Loo, having reported the case to the supreme government at Peking, received an imperial edict, requiring him to order the Hong merchants to command the remaining members of the factory to send a letter to their country, so that other taepans might be sent to Canton to control the affairs of commerce as hitherto. This imperial edict was obeyed, as it appears from the records of my office.

During the eleventh month of the Current year (the 16th of Taou-kwang), I received a petition from the English barbarian Elliot (Eluh) at Macao, in which he stated: 'Having received a despatch from my country, requiring me to proceed to Canton in an official capacity, to control my country's merchants and seamen there; and at the same time there being many ships in port, and many merchants and seamen in Canton and at Whampoa, who are ignorant of the laws of the Celestial Empire; and being really afraid that troubles may arise, I beg to be permitted to go to the Provincial City to control them.' The phrase, 'official capacity,' used in the petition, is equivalent to 'barbarian chief,' wholly different from that of taepan.

With a view to ascertain what might be the official capacity of the said barbarian: whether he really came for the simple purpose of controlling the merchants and seamen, not to regulate the trade; and whether he had any credentials from his country—these points not being sufficiently manifest—I immediately despatched a messenger, in company of Hong merchants, to Macao, there, in concert with the local, civil and military functionaries to investigate the matter.

On his return the messenger reported, that he had executed his commission, and examined the several points in regard to the same barbarian Ellut, who deposed as follows:—'My name is Elliot; I am an English officer of the fourth rank; in the autumn of the 14th year of Taou-kwang, I arrived here on a cruiser, which was duly reported by the pilots. During the two years whilst residing at Macao, I have been engaged in signing the passports of the English ships bound homewards. And now the Company's factory is not re-established, and no taepans arrived; but having a despatch from the great ministers of my king, directing me to control the merchants and seamen, and not to manage their commercial affairs, and also credentials; I am instructed thereby to proceed to the city in an official capacity; and in case of difficulties among the merchants or seamen, to control them, &c.'

Moreover, the messenger ascertained that the said barbarian, Elliot, brought

27

with him one wife and a child, and that they all were then resident in Macao; and that all the foreign merchants of other countries, as well as those of his own, testified that Elliot was a very quiet man, who attended only to his own affairs. Such was the messenger's report.

'Upon examination, I find that, since, the dissolution of the English Company's factory, no taepans have arrived here; that, for the last year, the said barbarian Elliot has been engaged at Macao in signing the manifests of English ships homeward bound, and quietly attending to his business; that the arrival of ships from his country being frequent, and the merchants and seamen numerous, it is necessary without delay to have someone to oversee and keep them in order; that the said barbarian has received credentials from his country with instructions to control its merchants and seamen; and that he is really the same as the taepans, though the name be different, it merely substituting one barbarian for another, which change, as it leads to no evil consequences, I suppose may be allowed.

In accordance with the regulations for the taepans, who were permitted to come to the Provincial City to transact their business, I have ordered the said barbarian to remain at Macao, till I have represented the case to court, hoping that by the Imperial favour, his request will be granted. Thereupon I will confer with the Hoppo, and direct him to issue a passport for Elliot to come to the Provincial City, that in future he may reside alternately in Macao, and Canton, according to the old regulations; but in the going and coming he must not exceed the limits, loitering about or protracting his stay in Canton. And again, I will issue orders to the civil and military officers, and to the Hong merchants to keep a constant watch over him; and if at any time he departs from his duty, or enters into plots with traitorous natives, or by any secret schemes contravenes the laws, they must instantly expel him from the country, in order at once to eradicate the roots of the evil.

Whether it be right or not to grant his request and adopt these regulations; I earnestly beg his Sacred Majesty to determine; and for this purpose I present this memorial; I wait for my instructions.' [18c]

The answer of the Emperor arrived in a short time, short in conformity with Chinese reckoning of time, and he was pleased to agree with the request of Captain Elliot. From the Emperor the permit was communicated by the Viceroy to the Hoppo, and by him transmitted to the Hong Merchants, in an order dated 18th March.[24a] That gentleman, therefore, proceeded immediately to Canton where he was welcomed, on 12th April, by cheers from English and other Europeans alike. Once more, by Elliot's hands this time, the British flag was hoisted on the staff before the factory,[18b] and he wrote his friend Conyngham that it was surely much easier to get on in China than into that nation.

In accordance with his 'orders,' Elliot remained in Canton about three weeks and then returned to Macao. During those three weeks, Captain Elliot's despatches to Lord Palmerston were filled with accounts of his vain attempts to procure a direct exchange of documents, even as between superior and inferior, between the Viceroy and himself. The Viceroy's orders, embellished with phrases indicating his low esteem of the taepan, were sent, as always, to the Hong merchants who relayed them to Elliot. To his friend, Lennox Conyngham, the Superintendent confided that, personally, he was satisfied with the results of his efforts to get into China and to get on with the Chinese authorities, that he had had a quarter-deck education and knew how to duck his head in a storm and hope for fairer weather; he expressed the hope that the British Government would, upon the whole, be satisfied with his conduct and see the situation as he did. But Palmerston did not and, upon receipt of Elliot's reports, the Foreign Secretary repeatedly sent instructions that communications were to be exchanged direct with the Viceroy and, under no circumstances, to be sent or received through the Hong Merchants, and that the form of petition was not to be used.[24b] It was November before Captain Elliot received these instructions from Palmerston and, immediately and repeatedly, he made attempts to find a form of procedure that would carry out his instructions and at the same time be acceptable to the Chinese.[VII] But the Viceroy was inexorable and Elliot reported this to the Foreign Office suggesting that a show of force, perhaps a letter from Palmerston to the cabinet at Peking, written by the Queen's command, and delivered to the mouth of the Peiho in a ship-of-war, might move the Son of Heaven to a concession on the one point, exchange of communications. But study of the correspondence that passed between Elliot and Palmerston yields little of moment, especially as to just what Elliot was supposed to do. Palmerston disapproved of his petitions and told him as much; but he failed to tell him how to avoid the consequences, for only refusal to receive 'orders' from above through the Hong merchants would have been Elliot's alternative. The British Government made no adequate statement of policy; Elliot did not know that he could count on armed support, nor did he have authority to deal with the drug traffic. He was, apparently, to see that the tea trade continued smoothly but, like the officials before him, to shut his eyes to smuggling. Daily the situation became more explosive. Even the British cutters became braver and carried their opium chests up into the river. When only the Chinese had landed the drug, the importers kept in the background and the former Superintendents could use the cloak of the late Company and allege that their business was to supervise the tea trade. But, in Elliot's early term, with the British boats engaged in direct smuggling on the outskirts of the

VII Elliot tried to substitute the unofficial letters, 'Shusin' or 'Sin,' for the form of petition.

provincial capital, it was impossible for Elliot to ignore the practice. Furthermore, he was distressed because the preventive police attempted to seize these boats; for he knew that, one day, serious trouble was due. His fears were well founded.

Captain Elliot appears to have resided in Macao from December 1836 until the second following August. Perhaps it was during these months, the only tranquil months of his years in China, that he worked on his contemporary pictures, drawings, and water-colours, which are said to be well composed and topographically most informing. The site of Portuguese Macao and the surrounding sea life undoubtedly offered much stimulation to artists.

In August 1838, Elliot returned to Canton to explain to the Chinese Authorities the approaching and friendly visit to Canton of Rear Admiral Sir Frederick Maitland. The Chinese still insisted on the use of the 'Pin' character signifying inferiority, so Elliot failed to communicate. Maitland, in H.M.S. *Wellesley*, a ship of the line, consequently called at Macao, and, in pursuance of instructions from the Admiralty to show the flag, sailed as far as the Tiger's mouth or Bogue's entrance, and left in September. Then, in December, the foreign factories, during an inflammatory phase in the opium smuggling, were actually for several hours in the hands of a riotous mob. Moreover, the Chinese authorities had determined to search all British boats suspected of this traffic and Elliot had determined to accompany the Chinese inspectors to the boat station in order to be on hand to protect the innocent traders.

On 31st December, 1838, the Emperor appointed Lin Tse-hsu as Imperial Commissioner to Canton with full authority to inspect the offices of the Viceroy, the Governor, and other officials, and to give all orders that he might deem necessary for the eradication of the opium traffic forever. It was rumoured throughout the Empire that even the Viceroy fell in a swoon when he read of his Emperor's determination to end the traffic; the Viceroy's boats carried the forbidden drug. Slippery and wise old Houqua, the senior Hong merchant, told Elliot that Lin would force the British to stop the opium smuggling by stopping the legitimate trade. Elliot said England would regard such action as not only unjust but hostile!

On 18th March, 1839, the Imperial Commissioner, who had arrived in Canton on 10th March, issued his edict. All opium owned by the barbarians was to be delivered to the Government; the Hongs were to draw up lists of parties concerned and the number of chests in their possession; foreigners were to give a future-conduct bond that their vessels would never again

30

bring in opium and that, if any were found after search, the parties were willing to suffer the death penalty. By 10th March, when Elliot, thinking that the first blow would fall on the shipping outside the river, had gone to Macao, war was in the air. Tents had been pitched, Chinese soldiers were assembling, and some old native vessels had been outfitted as fire-ships to force the opium ships at the entrance of the Bay of Hong Kong to concentrate at Macao. On 19th March, the Hoppo issued an order prohibiting egress from Canton and, on 22nd March, Mr Lancelot Dent, of the firm of Dent and Company, second largest opium importer, was summoned, purportedly by Lin, as hostage. Even the Hong merchants were, as an indication of degradation from official rank, deprived of their buttons and Houqua and Mowqua, the Chief Hongs, had chains placed around their necks.[24c]

A copy of Lin's edict reached Elliot, at Macao, the 22nd, and he immediately notified all British vessels at the outer anchorages to proceed to Hong Kong, hoist their national colours, be prepared to resist any aggression of the Chinese Government, and to be placed under the orders and protection of H.M. ships-of-war then in the China Seas.[24d] On 23rd March, the Superintendent ordered all British ships to prepare for attack, warned the Viceroy of the consequences, and ordered all British subjects to leave Canton.[24d] That same day he left Macao, reaching Whampoa at 4 p.m. There he learned that communications between that point and Canton had been severed for the past 48 hours. Captain Elliot donned his uniform and, with the Chinese passport for the cutter *Louise* in hand, proceeded, in the gig of H.M. sloop *Larne*, ensign and pennant hoisted, to the dwelling of the chief local Mandarin. This potentate tried in vain to dissuade the Superintendent from continuing into Canton. At 6 p.m. on the 24th, Elliot reached the factories and hoisted the British flag. The whole foreign community cheered. Some, who had already offered the Imperial Commissioner to surrender 1,030 chests of opium, wondered if they had been too hasty. Elliot next had Dent located and placed under his personal protection in his official residence.[VIII]

On 25th March, Captain Elliot demanded, and was refused, passports for British subjects. The next day, Lin refused clearance of ships and ordered that, first, all opium must be given up. Upon receipt of this demand by Lin, Captain Elliot, beginning to fear for the safety of the men and ships of his country, wrote Lin, expressing his regret for any disrespectful language he might have used and asking only that servants

---

VIII The former hall of the East India Company, since become the headquarters of the Superintendents.

and provisions be allowed to come in to the British in Canton. On 26th March, that same day, Lin repeated his demands, the delivery of the opium and giving of bonds, and warned against delay.

Elliot could evade no longer. The Chinese had learned, in December, that the Superintendent could be forced to stop opium smuggling within the river. Elliot had then issued a public notice to all British subjects: ordering boats engaged in illicit opium traffic to proceed outside the Bogue; warning British subjects engaged in opium smuggling that if a Chinese were killed, such British subjects were liable to capital punishment; withdrawing protection from smuggling boats when seized; and warning such craft that forcible resistance to search and seizure was a lawless act.[24e] Now they found that he could be forced to exercise control over the trade outside. So, a few hours after he had attempted a firm attitude, Elliot found himself reduced to informing the Chinese authorities that he would —because he together with all the British merchants and those of the other foreign nations settled at Canton were without food, servants, or intercourse with their home countries—deliver over all the opium in the hands of British subjects. In view of the situation, therefore, Elliot posted in the name of Her Majesty, a bold demand requiring surrender to him of all British-owned opium, 27th March. The demand was promptly answered, 28th March, in the surrender of 20,283 chests, worth at cost prices ten or 11 millions of dollars.[24f] The High Commissioner was so informed and, then, immediately, he turned pressure towards the American, French, and Dutch merchants whose opium trade, he declared, was no less than that of the English. But, on being informed that the opium in their hands was on English account and had been included in Elliot's report, Lin made no further demands on the other foreign merchants.

Yet, as Captain Elliot in his mistrust of the Chinese had feared, the immediate result of his submission was a tightening of constraint, even though Lin promised relaxation. From 28th March, three of the four streets leading into the British factory grounds were walled up, the back doors of the factories were bricked up, all foreigners' boats were hauled up on shore, guards were strengthened, and, each day, two buckets of spring water were delivered to each factory. By 2nd April, Lin, realizing that delivery of the opium would require a bit of time, ordered that food and water be supplied but that they should be cut off immediately at any sign of delay. Also, when the first fourth of the opium had been delivered, the compradors and servants should be restored; for the second fourth, communication with Whampoa and Macao; for the third fourth,

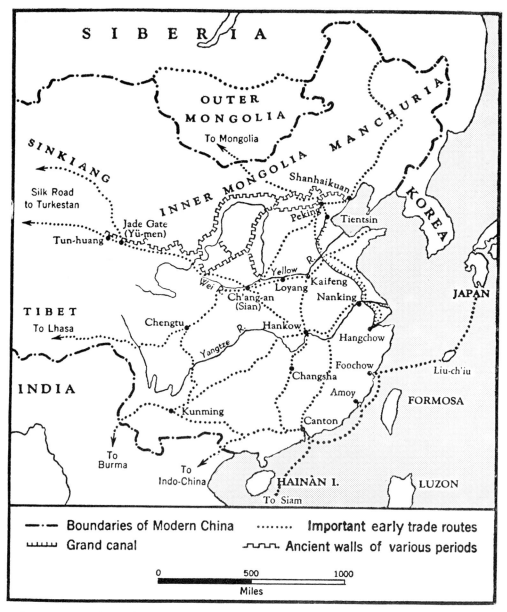

Important early trade routes (Fairbank, John King, *The United States and China*. Cambridge: Harvard University Press, 1948)

Harbour of Macao (Downing, C. Toogood, *The Fan-Qui in China in 1836–7*, II. London: Henry Colburn, 1838)

the embargo on trade should be removed; and, when the final fourth was delivered, business as originally conducted would be resumed.

Meanwhile, the question of the bond, against future trade in opium, had been presenting additional complications. On 25th March, a considerable number of the foreign merchants had signed such a bond as a personal pledge but this was unsatisfactory to Lin who wished that the entire foreign community sign. On 4th April, he demanded a collective bond and, on 5th and 8th April, the General Chamber of Commerce met for consideration of the new demand. On 8th April, upon deciding that the whole situation in China had assumed a political and not a commercial aspect, the Chamber dissolved. Finally, on 21st April, the bond again was brought to Captain Elliot who rejected it, saying he would sooner give his life than sign.

On 21st May, the delivery of 20,291 chests of opium was completed [24g] and, the next day, Elliot issued a protest [24g] against the unjustifiable imprisonment of the whole foreign community in Canton and the forced surrender of property. On 22nd May, the Superintendent ordered the British to leave Canton and prohibited British ships to enter. The following day, 23rd May, the High Commissioner and the Viceroy issued a joint order to the Hong merchants requiring 16 reputed principal opium importers to sign a promise to leave Canton forever. Elliot, fearing that refusal would serve as a pretext for further detention, recommended that these individuals sign and they did so, under duress. The next day, Elliot, accompanied by all British subjects who had not already left, departed for Macao.

The surrendered opium, 20,291 chests, was stored at Chenkow, near Chuenpee, and the High Commissioner, Viceroy, and Governor proposed to send the whole to Peking but the Emperor ordered that it should be destroyed on the spot. That way all foreigners and coastal inhabitants would see and hear and learn to tremble at Chinese authority. The *Chinese Repository* recorded the destruction—the opium was mixed with lime, salt, and water and flowed into the China Seas; but the June *Repository*, immediately following the British exodus from Canton, reported that the operations in opium had been renewed by vessels trading along the coast. [24h]

By July, Elliot was concerned with the formidable organization of the native smugglers and the vigorous trade being carried on to the east of Canton. [24i] And Elliot was, in fact, powerless in Macao, though, through the interference of the Foreign Office with the Lisbon Government, difficulties in the way of correspondence between the Portuguese authorities and the British commissioners had been alleviated. [27a] During the 1839 crisis, the difficulties in the way of regarding Macao as an adequately secure base for British commerce in China became glaringly apparent. For example, Elliot had been unable to arrest an alleged buccaneer who took harbour in Macao; Elliot, moreover, had often protested the vexatious treatment suffered by British subjects in the Portuguese management of customs affairs. Then, too, Elliot realized that the Governor, if possible, intended to preserve Portugal's neutrality.

A pertinent incident occurred in the first week of July 1839. Foreign sailors, on the east shore anchorage in Hong Kong Bay, were engaged in a riot in which a Chinese named Lin Wei-hi was killed.[24j] As the result of the issue by the Superintendent of a notice offering a reward for the apprehension of the murderers, six men were tried according to English law, were found guilty of riot and assault, and sentenced to fines and imprisonment for periods varying from three to six months. In October, the six were sent to Singapore. The Chinese, however, wanted one executed for the one Chinese killed and, most of all, the Imperial Commissioner wanted an excuse for an interruption of the trade and, subsequently, for placing the blame for the state of commercial stagnation upon foreign shoulders rather than his own. The unavenged death of Lin Wei-hi supplied exactly the excuse. Lin threatened to move down with two thousand troops towards Macao and again, 16th August, servants were taken from the British. Elliot, to relieve pressure on the Portuguese Government of Macao, removed himself to the ship *Fort William* and, by September, all British subjects to Hong Kong. The Merchant fleet, strengthened by the arrival of H.M.S. *Volage*—a 28-gun frigate from India—Lord Auckland's answer to Elliot's letter for protection, was put in a state of defence. Lin entered Macao in a triumphal parade and ordered the Governor to watch for opium contrabandists and never again to permit the English to return to the town.[27b] But Lin left and Elliot petitioned the Governor that he and his countrymen be allowed to return to Macao and promised 1,000 men if the Governor ever feared for the safety of his town. The Macao Government replied that, though it had not turned the English out of its town, after Lin's promises, it had no power to allow their return. So, during the quieter weeks that followed, the British trickled back into Macao as they had entered—unofficially. But, even with Portuguese concurrence, Elliot and the British community had realized that Macao was of minor use to British commerce in China and that British ships needed a sea base where they could enjoy protection and freedom from Portuguese, or other foreign, situations. From such attitude was born Elliot's desire to acquire Hong Kong in British sovereignty.

The aim of Elliot's policy, during the winter of 1839-40, was to keep the trade going and, awaiting orders from his home government, to refrain from action. The end of August was the time when the main fleet of merchantmen always arrived and the following months were ones of the greatest commercial activity. Elliot knew, too, that the local government could not stop British trade without disturbing the peace of the southern provinces where millions of Chinese depended upon it for their very existence. Later, in June 1840, he confided to Lennox Conyngham that this was his strategy during those precarious months and that, surely, such would be sufficient answer to his critics. Captain Elliot's authority for what he did was questioned at Canton, at Macao, and in England, both in the country and in Parliament. But as his government continued the policy to which his acts inevitably led and, even though the question of the limits of his authority is an interesting one, it appears today, over a century away, that the necessity and wisdom of his actions are of paramount concern. The trade, Elliot reasoned, for centuries past, had been confined to Canton, both because the town was at the extremity of the Empire and because of its assumed impregnability. Consequently, he was convinced that, one day, England would have to prove to China that Canton was quite vulnerable, even in a three days' campaign. On their part, the merchants at Canton were, naturally, of diverse opinion. Amongst both American and English, some abstained from dealing in opium on conscientious grounds but even these agreed with their fellows, who were untroubled by conscientious scruples, that international relations required readjustment. Generally, the Americans were content to meet all of China's requirements and maintain a profitable face of neutrality; this they could safely do, so long as England fought the battle of the West. The English at Canton had long been pronounced in pointing out their opinion that, to effect any reforms, it was demands, not petitions, that must be presented to the Chinese Government. Many regarded Elliot's policy as weak and ineffective. The British Government, for its part, had neglected formulating a policy. In 1833, it had completely transformed the conditions of British trade at Canton, substituting what evolved into anarchism for the autocratic control of the Company; and it failed to provide machinery for regulating the old trade under new conditions. Repeated requests were sent, during five years, by the several Superintendents for instructions and for increased authority. All they received, after months of waiting, were injunctions not to exceed their authority, long despatches about proper ways to address the Chinese authorities, and instructions not to interfere with the operations of the merchants. To the Chinese, opium was the one reason for war, and in this just cause they expected the support of the whole Western World against England. Commissioner Lin had written [IX, 24k] and admonished the young Queen Victoria that he could detect no other cause than opium for the difficulties between China and England—that, indeed, the Court of Heaven had offered tea, silk, and rhubarb to England, and England, in turn, had permitted a tribe of depraved, barbarous pirates to sell a deadly poison into the Celestial Empire. Such a letter to a country whose Parliament, in 1832, did not deem it advisable to abandon so important a source of revenue as the Company's monopoly of opium in Bengal—a country where public opinion, in 1839, soon after his arrival home, returned Trader Jardine, the Opium King, as a Member of Parliament! The humanitarianism, which had triumphed with the abolition in 1833 of slavery in the British dominions, and which had rushed forward before Wilberforce and Raffles, was slower in its advance before opium.

In China, by the 1830's, certainly by 1838, so many of the native office-holding class were sharing, or hoped to share, in the wealth that flowed out of the Canton trade that, perhaps, only a very few individuals in officialdom had any desire to abolish the trade in opium. But the Emperor, who as the Son of Heaven embodied in his own person the legislative and judicial branches of the Chinese Imperial Government, honestly did desire the opium trade's end. Taokwang succeeded, in 1820, to a rotten court, a disorganized and corrupt government, and an empire rife with rebellion and disorder. His court he reformed, the government he tried and failed to reform by edicts, and his empire he saw become the scene of disasters and insurrections that increased in frequency and in violence with each year of his reign. And, of all his individual problems, none exceeded in importance the opium question. Taokwang was an earnest man but his task was hopeless. Acquiescence, both Chinese and foreign, in the prohibitory opium law could be obtained only temporarily and locally.

By October of 1839, a stage of compromise was reached and, on the 20th, the Superintendent notified the British merchants that, without signing the debated bond, their ships could proceed to the Chuenpee anchorage and enter into trade on the same terms, as to payment of Chinese dues and examination of cargo, as if their ships were at Whampoa.[24l] Then the episode of the *Thomas Coutts* occurred, an act which is generally recognized as having inspired the High Commissioner to revive the battle.

The *Thomas Coutts*, a British merchantman, had arrived at Macao on 13th October and her master, Warner, was one of that independent brand of Englishmen of whom the number is large. Warner considered Elliot's

IX Lin's letter to Victoria is preserved in the *Chinese Repository*, January 1840, and interpreted by Morse, *International Relations*.

order forbidding British ships to go up to Canton as untenable; on his way to the China Seas, Warner had secured this legal opinion in Calcutta. As he was, furthermore, outside the opium ring and had no fears from that quarter, Warner, on 15th October, applied to the Chinese for permission to trade, duly signed the opium bond, which carried express consent to submit to capital punishment and entire confiscation of ship and cargo, readily received his permit, and took his ship straightway to Whampoa. Warner's recklessness undid all that Elliot had striven for; it put a British ship and a British crew into Lin's itching palm.

The three days 25th to 27th October witnessed Lin's reply. During those several days, Elliot, at Macao, received the High Commissioner's Orders for the surrender of the murderer of Lin Wei-hi; that the ships should either enter or sail away within three days, under penalty of complete destruction by fire; that, with the cargoes accumulated through half a year of stoppage of trade, lightering from Chuenpee to Canton would consume too much trade—the British *Thomas Coutts* and the American *Mermaid* both had signed the required bond and entered the river—why should not all ships do likewise? Furthermore, Lin resumed, attempt to stop neither the opium traffic nor the resulting homicides along the coast had been made; if Elliot refused to do his duty, Chinese war vessels [x] would proceed to Hong Kong and carry out the High Commissioner's orders.[24m]

Many a foreigner in China began to ask if China were to have a Black Hole of Calcutta. But, apparently, Lin made a profound mistake in his ignorant and wishful thinking, not only about the power of the naval force opposed to him but of the reinforcement from England that it would receive. Even the Hong merchants and the lowly wharf coolies were more realistic than the High Commissioner.

Upon receipt of Lin's order, the alternative to enter the river or be destroyed, Captain Elliot wrote to Captain H. Smith of H.M.S. *Volage*,[28a] acquainting him with recent circumstances, saying that the liberty, lives, and properties of the Queen's subjects were menaced, and ordering Smith to collect the merchant fleet and ride at anchorage below Chuenpee at a point called Tong-ku and himself move to the Bogue mouth on the *Volage* with the *Hyacinth*, 20 guns, but newly arrived.[24n] On 28th October, Elliot joined Smith on board the *Volage*, then made fast at Macao. In company with the *Hyacinth*, the two British ships sailed to the Bogue at Chuenpee, which point, though but 50 miles distant, was not reached until 2nd November as the wind was strongly adverse.[28a] Both ships anchored a mile below the

---

x Elliot knew that Lin had been assembling a force of war-junks and fire-rafts.

battery, from which an imposing force of war-junks and fire-boats was observed some eight miles away in the mouth of the river. This was the Chinese provincial fleet, under Admiral Kuan T'ien-p'ei, for no Chinese navy existed; it consisted of 29 vessels, 15 being men-of-war and 14 fire-boats. Even though the merchantmen had guns, a sudden night attack with fire-boats such as the Chinese possessed was capable of doing great damage to the merchantmen. Captain Elliot, realizing this, determined to deflect Lin, either by reason or force, as Lin had plainly stated his intention to destroy the merchant fleet, if his orders were not obeyed.

There followed an exchange of notes between the Captain of the *Volage* and the Chinese Admiral and, early on the morning of 3rd November, the Chinese squadron broke ground and stood out towards H.M.'s ships which were immediately got under weigh and directed towards the approaching force. But, soon, the squadron of 29 sail, instead of continuing its course, came to anchor in a line stretching to the southward from Chuenpee point, a manœuvre which indicated that it was neither going to attack nor expected to be attacked. H.M.'s ships hove to and Captain Smith sent a note to Admiral Kuan asking that the Chinese withdraw. The Admiral replied by demanding from Elliot the murderer of Lin Wei-hi.

The whole responsibility now rested on Elliot. He knew that the Admiral's reply was sheer subterfuge. Lin Wei-hi was a Chinese villager who had been killed in an affray at Kow-loon nearly six months before, and Elliot had again and again assured the Emperor's High Commissioner that Wei-hi's death could not be fastened upon any of the British sailors concerned in the riot. As for Smith, Elliot knew only too well what he advised: sink the whole Chinese fleet! But this Elliot could not sanction as the Chinese, after their first threatening gesture of standing towards the British, had come to anchor. But there was Lin's ultimatum—submit or be annihilated. Elliot knew well all the attitudes, except that in London. He had no intimation of the Cabinet's attitude toward any of the grave events in China in 1839. Perhaps the Cabinet still desired, at any cost, peace in the Far East. Should he, therefore, be the individual to precipitate armed conflict between England and China? If he did, would he be upheld or repudiated and even cashiered and ruined? It required, at best, four months to get an answer from England and this alone was enough to make a man act on his own initiative. The British Empire, Elliot knew, had been largely built by men on the scene who, without time for instructions, did the appropriate thing.

But Captain Smith felt no such responsibilities as Elliot. He was, by now, disgusted with the Chinese and the Admiral's irrelevant demand was, he told Elliot, only a stall. The Chinese squadron would pass inside him during

38

the night and annihilate the merchantmen, which were at anchor a mile below the first battery. Feeling it incompatible with the honour of the flag to retire, Smith, at noon of 3rd November, gave the signal to engage. The Chinese replied with a spirited fire. The two frigates, *Hyacinth* and *Volage*, were hove to near the south end of the Chinese warships which were, as before, at anchor in a north-south line and at right angles to the direction of the wind. Smith's ships, the *Volage* leading, bore away in close order, both wind and Chinese on their starboard beam and, thus, under easy sail, ran up the Chinese line, at 50 yards distance, pouring in on their port beam. A fire-boat went down; then a warship blew up. The two frigates continued their devastating sail northward. Reaching the top of the line, they turned and ran down it, now their larboard broadsides blazing. The Chinese, caught at anchor by the sudden onset, had weighed or slipped or cut by now and began to scatter as best they could. Some were deserted by their crews who took to the small boats and rowed away. Not so the Admiral. Elliot forever remembered that Chinese officer's admirable conduct. In all the hopelessness of the situation, Admiral Kuan T'ien-p'ei bore up and engaged Her Majesty's Ships in such handsome style that, finally, when he was forced to break off action and in a water-logged condition was attempting to make for shore, the *Hyacinth*, which was ranging alongside, was ordered not to sink him. At the end of the 45 minute Battle of Chuenpee, the Chinese suffered the loss of four men-of-war junks with most of their other vessels so holed up and dismasted that they could not have reached the Bogue had not Elliot ordered Smith to cease fire. On their part, the Chinese guns, which apparently could neither be raised nor lowered, failed to score a single hit on the hulks of the frigates, which had sustained damage only to their rigging and only one sailor from their crews wounded. Smith sailed away to Macao, after Elliot asked the merchantmen to rendezvous at Tong-ku, which he considered a safe anchorage. Thus, on 3rd November 1839, in the Battle of the Chuenpee, the flower of the Celestial Empire's fleet, in a brief encounter with two British frigates of the second and third class, first tasted the bitter warfare of 19th-century Europe.

While these events had been occurring in the China Seas, at very long last, the British Government at home was beginning to turn its attention to China policy. Except for the brief interval 1834-35 when the office was filled by the Duke of Wellington in Peel's Tory administration, Palmerston had been Foreign Secretary since 1830. By the time of the Battle of Chuenpee in China, Palmerston was the greatest figure in all England, far overshadowing Prime Minister Lord Melbourne, and noted for his dash and tact, his pleasantness and resolution; and, also, noted for his highly meddlesome policy in Europe and, recently, even in Asia, for he had invaded Afghanistan. So the merchant princes, trading to China and led by William Jardine, had come to believe, by 1839, that in Palmerston they had a man who could readily be pressed to adopt a vigorous Chinese policy. These influential British traders, some since the days when the ill-fated Macartney and Amherst missions had striven in vain to break down the old China closed system of commercial intercourse, had long held the view that a demonstration in force would teach China a lesson and over-come the Imperial Court's objection to a free trade. So the traders pressed the Foreign Office.

In the last months of 1839, the bulk of the correspondence between the Superintendents and the Foreign Office, from Napier's appointment to the end of 1839, was collected and printed and the British Government, in the early spring of 1840, laid its policy before Parliament.[XI] The great opium debate in the Commons followed. In reply to a question in the Commons on 19th March, 1840, Lord Palmerston claimed that the object of Britain's warlike preparations was threefold: to obtain reparation for insults suffered by the Superintendent and other subjects of Her Majesty, an indemnity for the loss of merchants' property, and future security for British traders.[10a] On 7th April, a motion of censure on the Government was moved and, after a very vocal and lengthy debate, was defeated by the narrow majority of nine in a house of 533 members.[10a] The debate, which covered as much detail as the orators could muster, had ranged over the period from 1833 to 1840. The members knew, by early March of 1840, most of the events in China up to the loudly rumoured fight at Chuenpee. Even Palmerston and Lord John Russell, Secretary for the Colonies, knew nothing reliable of that event until the official account arrived near the close of March. Some members of the opposition boldly put the opinion that war had, Parliament unknowing, been declared against China. Sir Robert Peel, opposition leader, asked whether, should the rumour be true about a war, it was to be an imperial war or merely an armed demonstration only by the Government of India. Palmerston was harangued as to the exact instructions that had been sent to China and as to what course would be adopted about compensation for the seized opium. Accordingly, a motion was drafted to the effect that the interruption of commercial intercourse with China and the hostile clashes that had followed were due to the Cabinet's want of foresight, especially to the neglect of instructing Captain Elliot how to cope with the contraband traffic, which had got out of hand

---

XI This vast material was printed in *Correspondence and Papers Relating to China*, a White Paper laid before Parliament early in 1840.

and endangered the legitimate trade. Looking back over a century, this appears to be the truth.

By the last days of March 1840, England was thick with rumours and the press was full of criticisms. Several members insisted that the preparations then going on in India were warlike preparations and Palmerston, pressed as to the object and date of such an expedition, restated his threefold object in China: to obtain reparations for insults, indemnification for wrongful losses of merchants' property, and security for future trade. This answer satisfied the House until wary members said the Foreign Secretary's objects covered a demand for the value of the seized opium and therefore that the war, in part certainly, would be an opium war, should war occur. Then the situation in Parliament developed rapidly. In reform and humanitarian circles, in the High Church party and the 'Saints,' the idea of a war to uphold the opium trade was repugnant and, ordinarily, it was this reform and humanitarian group which supported Palmerston's Whig administration. Also, a large section of the commercial class, angered at the Government's clumsy endangering of trade, was indignant.

But, all the while, Palmerston had held the trump card, insult to the flag and attempts on the lives and liberties of Her Majesty's subjects. And, to reply for the Government, Palmerston had no small support in the Secretary of State for War, Thomas Babington Macaulay. The young but powerful orator was already famous as a writer, his essays having, by 1840, mostly appeared, though the *Lays* and the *History of England* were yet to come. Besides, he had been an M.P. during 1830-34 and, again, since 1839; and those four years, 1834-38, as member on the Supreme Council of India, had given him an aura of esteem on Eastern affairs unenjoyed by most other members. Macaulay began his able defence of the Government by saying that the motion of censure was concerned with the past, not the present, and that no word in the mover's speech criticized the Government's present policy to exact reparation and obtain a settled trade. He went on to point out that, in circumstances where letters took six months to arrive, it was useless to send detailed instructions because, before they could be received, the situation the instructions were devised to meet might have altered. Every Briton knew that the great men who built the Empire had the spirit to treat all orders from home as waste paper. Had they not done so there would be no Empire. Lord Palmerston's orders were ample; Captain Elliot had not been told to bring the opium trade under control as no power or authority vested in him would have given him the power to do so. If England could not control brandy and tobacco smuggling into England herself, what sort of staff would Captain

41

Elliot have to have to control opium smuggling into China? Then the eloquent orator launched into a typical Macaulayan description of the barbarous Lin's policies, of his demand for innocent blood, and of his driving from their homes of women with child and of children at the breast. Captain Elliot, Macaulay continued, had touched him personally and deeply when, on Elliot's arrival at the factory in Canton, he was surrounded by a group of his agonized and despairing countrymen and, to revive these poor souls and let them know that he, their protector, had arrived, he ordered the flag of Great Britain to be taken from his boat and to be planted in the factory balcony. Only then could those poor souls be reminded that they belonged to a country unaccustomed to defeat, submission or shame—a country which made the farthest ends of the earth ring with the fame of her exploits in redressing the wrongs of her children —a country that made the Dey of Algiers humble himself to her insulted Consul—a country that revenged the Black Hole horrors on the fields of Plassey—a country that had not degenerated since her great Protector vowed that he would make the name of Englishman as respected as ever had been the name of Roman citizen. Englishmen in remote China looked homeward for protection. Concluding his oration, Macaulay pleaded that those men, to whom was entrusted the task of demanding reparations, might be successful but merciful, so that the name, not only of English valour, but of English mercy, might be established.

So was the House told, in glow and sentiment, that there was to be a war in China.

Even the young Gladstone, whom Macaulay had once called the rising hope of the stern and unbending Tories, could not, in all his righteous and moral indignation, make the Macaulay-swayed majority realize that the opium smuggled into China came exclusively from British ports, from Bengal and through Bombay. So was the motion of censure on the Government defeated by the narrow majority of nine in a house of 533.[10a]

Meanwhile, around 20th February 1840, Palmerston had written to the Government of India to prepare the armament which was to be placed at the disposal of the Plenipotentiaries in China. Admiral the Honourable George Elliot,[XII, 28b] a cousin of Captain Elliot, was given the naval command and, also, was empowered to act as plenipotentiary along with Captain Elliot [5a] in making claims upon the Chinese Government when the expedition arrived off Canton, which it should do by the end of

---

XII Admiral Elliot had won Nelson's high praise, served as one of the Lords Commissioners, and, since 1837, had been Commander-in-Chief of the Cape of Good Hope. On 15th February 1840, he was transferred to the chief command in the East Indies. See O'Byrne's *Naval Biographical Dictionary*, 533.

June.[XIII] The military force, under the command of General Burrell, was to consist of three regiments of infantry, a volunteer regiment of Indian troops, and two companies of sappers and miners. The naval armament consisted of three ships of 72 guns, two of over 40, five of 20 or more, six smaller vessels and four steamers.[27c] Governor-General Auckland had argued strongly for a complete blockade of Canton, the occupation of Chusan or one of its sister islands and an attack upon the Chinese junks, ports, and other property, but taking care not to damage the civilian population and their trade.[27c]

Meanwhile, on the other side of the world, the Battle of Chuenpee, 3rd November 1839, had left Captain Elliot victorious over the best Chinese fleet that Lin could send against him. The events of Chuenpee Lin represented to Court as merely another example of the disgraceful conduct of Outer Barbarians. In Europe such naval action would have created war between the involved nations; not so, in China. In Chinese political thought, war did not exist. Since the Son of Heaven ruled all the world, the skirmish at Chuenpee was a civil breach of the peace and occurred when the Celestial authorities had to punish the Foreign Devils, because the centuries-old Chinese diplomacy of soothing and admonishing had, for once, not worked too well. Lin's triumph in getting the opium had made him too certain of his continued triumph. But, after Chuenpee, some of the Emperor's advisors began to fear and warn that Lin's actions would result in the very situation that China had always avoided—a greater rather than a lesser invasion by the Barbarians. Yet the Emperor, knowing nothing of the formidable expedition that was preparing in India, heard only Lin's platitudinous utterances and, between November 1839 and June 1840, when the expedition arrived, continued, as his illustrious ancestors before him had done, to lull himself into the wishful thought that the Son of Heaven ruled all the world.

At the same time, the British could do nothing until they were reinforced.[240] In December 1839, there were 32 merchantmen at anchor in Hong Kong and the road north of it, Tong-ku. They traded by transshipping their cargoes through the neutral Americans and the receipt of tea continued most gratifyingly. The merchants themselves and their families moved, during the post-Chuenpee period, sometimes to Macao and sometimes back to shipboard, according as tension decreased or increased. Furthermore, the drug traffic continued to thrive and the British in India continued to plant opium crops.

XIII The Government's approval of Captain Charles Elliot's proceedings thus far is shown by his appointment as plenipotentiary conjointly with his cousin.

43

Ostensibly, trade was at a standstill. On 20th November 1839, Captain Elliot gave notice that British ships would be forcibly prevented from entering the port of Canton. On 26th November, the High Commissioner retaliated by issuing orders that, after 6th December, no British ships would be allowed to enter; on 5th January 1840, he followed this up by a proclamation closing Canton 'forever' to British ships, the produce of Great Britain, or any of her dependencies.[240, p] In typical and refreshing Chinese fashion, Lin failed to take steps to prevent the continued introduction of the goods of the seafaring English in neutral bottoms. At Hong Kong and Tong-ku, the Chinese continued a petty and delaying, but otherwise harmless, annoyance to British ships but, otherwise, peace prevailed until June of 1840. During these months, Elliot's despatches to the Foreign Office were both strongly worded and lengthy.[2a, 3a] He gave full reports of the forcible detention of the Superintendent and the whole foreign community, the surrender of the opium, the withdrawal of the British merchants and the merchants' subsequent memorial, the Lin Wei-hi affair, the expulsion from Macao, the Chuenpee engagement, the embargo preventing British ships from entering the port, and the British continuance of trade in neutral bottoms. Elliot's despatches, to 29th May, were received at the Foreign Office from September 1840 through January 1841.[24q]

On 28th June 1840, Admiral George Elliot arrived in China as Senior Plenipotentiary [24p] and brought with him not only copies of Palmerston's instructions [27d] but a fleet of 16 men-of-war, four armed steamers of the East India Company, and 27 transport, carrying 4,000 Irish, Scottish, and Indian troops. The fleet consisted of three 74s, one of which, the *Melville* was flying the flag of Rear Admiral the Honourable George Elliot, Commander-in-Chief; two first-class frigates, 44s; three second-class, 28s; and eight sloops carrying from ten to 18 guns each. Colonel Burrell was in command of the land troops, with Colonel Oglander, who died at sea later on the way to Chusan, as second in command.[24r] This fleet, which Lin said was not going to venture disturbances but which would, like rats, enter Chinese waters to protect the base opium trade, assembled near Hong Kong.

The Foreign Secretary's instructions, which were dated 20th February 1840,[24s] ordered the two Elliots, as Joint Plenipotentiaries, immediately to occupy one of the Chusan group of islands, to communicate to some officer of the Chinese Government a letter from Palmerston to 'the Minister of the Emperor of China' and, then, to proceed to the mouth of the Peiho to sign a treaty with an accredited plenipotentiary of the Chinese Emperor.[27d] If satisfaction were not received, the chief ports and the two great rivers, the Yangtze Kiang and the Yellow, were to be blockaded until the demands of the British Government were conceded. In his personal letter to the Chinese Government, Palmerston deplored the violent outrages which had been committed against both British residents and the Queen's Officer in China; he stressed the necessity of an impartial administration of law and complained of a system in which officials from the Governor downwards annually enjoyed great profit from the opium trade. Then, continued the Foreign Secretary, the Chinese Government itself, instead of seizing the illegally imported opium, had laid hands on the persons of the Super-intendent and all British merchants, innocent and guilty, and starved them until the British Officer turned over the opium. Palmerston, therefore, demanded the repayment of the ransom; the communication 'in a manner consistent with usages of civilized nations' to the British Officer; the repayment by the Chinese Government of the debts owed by the Hong merchants, as it had granted exclusive rights to this monopolist body; and, finally, future security.[27d] For this last purpose, future security, one or more sufficiently large and properly situated islands on the coast was to be selected by the British Plenipotentiaries to be permanently given up to the British Government as a place of residence and commerce for its subjects.[27e] In closing his letter, Lord Palmerston stated that, if the time should come when questions of mutual concessions should arise, and if the Indian Government abandoned a direct interest in opium production, then the British Government would be disposed fairly to weigh such problems as the price of full reparation and the placing of commerce with China on a more liberal and satisfactory footing. Foreseeing such results, Palmerston said, personally, he was desirous of discouraging, on the part of British agents, extension of poppy cultivation.[27e] Along with the instructions and letter, a draft treaty, sent to the Plenipotentiaries, stipulated that British subjects of both sexes with the persons of their establishments should be allowed to reside at the five ports of Canton, Amoy, Foochow, Shanghai, and Ningpo; there, also, the British consuls or superintendents were to reside and enjoy both respect and direct communication with Peking; the Queen was to receive the cession of islands or an island to be designated by the British Plenipotentiaries— but, should the Chinese be reluctant to cede territory, the grant on the mainland was to be secured; a money equivalent for the destroyed opium, the ransom paid to preserve the lives of British hostages, was to be repaid; the Hong system monopoly was to be destroyed and the Hong debts paid; an agreement for the reimbursement of the expedition's expenses was included; successive stages of the relaxation of the British hold on Chinese territory and shipping was outlined; the treaty was to be drawn up in both languages, but the English text was to be authoritative; any prohibited articles were to be prohibited to all foreigners alike; the Chinese Government was to grant to all foreigners the same rights; Chinese authorities were authorized to confiscate any prohibited goods or lawful goods smuggled into China; the persons of British subjects were to be immune from molestation; if the Chinese Government strongly objected to the exportation of precious metals, British subjects might be debarred from receiving coin or bullion for the sale of their commodities (this was the only restriction, on the otherwise absolute freedom of commercial activities, to which Palmerston gave the Plenipotentiaries liberty to agree); the British Government was to be allowed to erect courts to try alleged British criminals and civil cases in which British subjects were the defendants; and, finally, the treaty was to be ratified by the Chinese Emperor and by Queen Victoria.[27e]

The *Chinese Repository* for July 1840 carried what may be considered the Chinese reply to the demands of the barbarians. In the shape of proclamations, issued under the authority of Commissioner Lin, rewards were offered for the capture and destruction of English ships, and the capture or death of English officers and men. For the capture of a ship-of-war, the captors were to receive all her contents, except armament and any opium on board, and, in addition, a cash bonus of $20,000 for an 80-gun ship, with a reduction of $100 for each gun less; for the destruction of a ship-of-war, half the above sums. For the capture of a merchant vessel, the captors were to receive her contents, except armament and opium, and a cash bonus of $10,000 for a ship, $5,000 for a barque, $3,000 for a brig or schooner, $300 for a large boat, and $100 for a small boat; for the destruction of any of these various types of boats, one-third of these respective sums. For the capture of a naval commander, $5,000, with a reduction of $500 for each step down in rank; for killing them, one-third of these sums. English soldiers, sailors, and merchants were valued at $100 each for capture and $40 each for killing; proportionate sums were established for sepoys and lascars. The capture of a Chinese traitor was to bring $100.[24t]

As 1840 progressed, Chinese irritation grew. On 25th February 1841, the Governor of Kwangtung offered much greater, and to Her Majesty's servants much more flattering, rewards:[24t]

For the capture of a ship of the line $100,000

For her destruction 30,000

For a frigate or sloop, in proportion

For capture of a large steamer 50,000
For capture of a small steamer 25,000
For capture alive of Elliot, Morrison, or Bremer, each ... 50,000
For their heads, each 30,000
For capture of an English officer 10,000
For his head 5,000
For capture of an English soldier or sailor 500
For his head 300
For capture of a sepoy or lascar 100
For his head 50
For those who lost their lives in effecting seizures, a gratuity
    to their families of 300

We recall that Elliot had received a letter from Palmerston for delivery to the Chinese Government. This letter had to be delivered even though, by 28th June 1840,[24u] the British had established the blockade of the Canton River and the first step for them to take, thereafter, would seem to have been to destroy the defences of the river. Thus, on 30th June, the two Plenipotentiaries, Admiral Elliot and Captain Elliot, Palmerston's letter in hand, sailed north with the warships. Some ships stopped near Amoy, 300 miles up the coast, and tried to send the letter ashore, under a flag of truce, to the authorities there. But the Chinese, ignorant of what the white flag meant, refused to allow any British sailors to land. The attempt was abandoned and the fleet proceeded on another 400 miles to Chusan Island, south of the estuary of the Yangtze River. On 4th July, Commander Bremer[5b] summoned Ting-hai, the chief city of the island, to surrender. When the Governor refused, the town was occupied, 5th July, by landing parties, the Chinese being quite unprepared to make any resistance.[24v] The Ting, the Chinese Civil Magistrate, committed suicide, the first of many such episodes which were to follow in the story of the opening of China and which were to excite various attitudes in the minds of the English—admiration, respect, even scorn. Meanwhile, Chusan was placed under a British administration, Doctor Charles Gutzlaff, the Prussian medical missionary from Macao, being made City Magistrate. On 10th July, the British made an attempt at Ningpo, similar to the unsuccessful one at Amoy, of sending Palmerston's letter to the Chinese Government. At Ningpo the white flag was respected, the letter-bearers were courteously treated, but the letter was refused. Having established a blockade of Ningpo and the mouth of the Yangtze, the fleet sailed on to the mouth of the Peiho, another 800 miles distance and within 100 miles of Peking. Here, finally, the letter was received by a Manchu dignitary, Grand Secretary Kishen, who also was Viceroy of the Metropolitan Province. As the letter had to be referred to the Emperor, the British agreed upon 27th August as a meeting date with the Chinese, and then they went for a cruise. [5c]

When Kishen presented Palmerston's letter to the Emperor, the Son of Heaven, realizing that Lin's policy had led to the barbarians arriving in force almost at the gates of the capital of the Celestial Empire, was infuriated at his trusted representative and sent him a violent letter of dismissal. Lin was summoned to Peking, tried, and exiled to Ili, a lonely frontier town in distant Sinkiang Province. Kishen was appointed Plenipotentiary to negotiate with the two barbarian Elliots. Subsequently, Charles Elliot informed the Chinese Government that the British Government was indifferent as to whether Lin were punished or not and, many months later, Palmerston praised Elliot for his attitude towards Lin's misfortune.[3b]

On the appointed date, 27th August, the British fleet returned to the mouth of the Peiho and, as there apparently was no communication from shore, prepared to force the passage of the Taku forts. But a letter arrived from Kishen, explaining his special position and suggesting that the second plenipotentiary, Captain Elliot, come ashore for a personal interview. The suggestion was accepted and the interview was held on 30th August.[24w] After a six-hour and loud discussion, Elliot returned to his ship, further reference was made to Peking, the British took another cruise, and, on 12th September, again returned to the Peiho. Kishen suggested that all should adjourn to Canton, the scene of all the difficulties to be settled and the source of the truth of the facts in dispute. The English Plenipotentiaries, assuring Kishen that, except under provocation, no further aggressive movement would be made, returned to their ships which, on 15th September, left the Peiho and returned to Chusan, arriving at Ting-hai on 28th September.[24x] There they were delayed and concerned by the health of the troops occupying the island and by an act of barbarity committed by the Chinese. Intermittent fever, diarrhoea, and dysentery had taken a toll of 448 deaths in a force of 4,000 and admissions to the hospital had numbered 5,329.[5d] Some of the sick had been sent to Manila whence, upon Spanish refusal of permission to land, they were taken to Hong Kong. Also, Captain Elliot was alarmed at the Chinese capture and mistreatment of Captain Anstruther of the Madras artillery, Lieutenant Douglas R.N., Commander of the armed brig *Kite*, and several other survivors from the *Kite*, including Mrs Noble, wife of the sailing-master. These individuals had been loaded with heavy leg-irons and forced into tiny cages which were exposed in the market-places of towns on the

Feasting the Grand Hoppo (Downing, C. Toogood, *The Fan-Qui in China in 1836–7*, III. London: Henry Colburn, 1838)

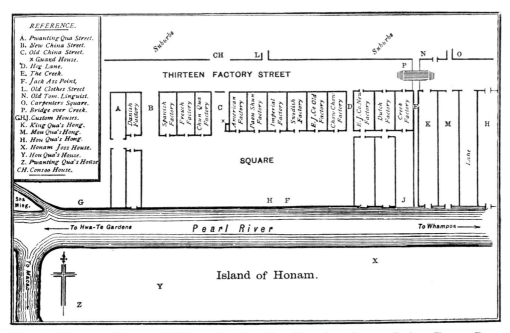

Island of Honam (Hunter, William C., *The 'Fan-Kwae' at Canton Before Treaty Days, 1825–1844*. London: Kegan, Paul, Trench & Co., 1882)

Peasants on Danes Island (Downing, C. Toogood, *The Fan-Qui in China in 1836–7*, I. London: Henry Colburn, 1838)

island. Elliot failed to secure release of these prisoners but secured promise of fair treatment. The British later learned that orders were received from Peking to execute the officers among these prisoners, all of which, ultimately, in February 1841, were released and brought south by the British troops evacuating Ting-hai in March.

The Plenipotentiaries sailed south, reaching Macao on 20th November. Their withdrawal from the very doors of the Emperor's Palace, when they were supported by a formidable fleet and force, was, of course, interpreted by the Chinese as barbarian weakness.[5e] Similarly was Admiral Elliot's early departure from Macao. Admiral Elliot, invalided for some weeks, was forced to resign the command of the fleet into the hands of Commodore Sir Gordon Bremer [5f] and, on 29th November, Charles Elliot was signing despatches as 'H.M.'s Plenipotentiary in China'. This, though only the signature shows it, left Captain Elliot as sole Plenipotentiary. Some accounts claim that the Admiral's illness was one of convenience, a result of irreconcilable differences of opinion between the cousins. If this be true, it is difficult to understand why the senior of two plenipotentiaries should withdraw in favour of his junior. At any rate, Admiral George Elliot was invalided home on board the *Volage* 26 and, from 1841, placed on half-pay and, subsequently, retired from public life.[5f] Of Charles Elliot the Admiral recalled that his cousin 'was associated with me in my diplomatic character as plenipotentiary, and no one was better versed than him in all Chinese interests, fears, objects and prejudices'. [5g]

Of the criticism that the two Elliots, supported by fleet and force, had reached the very outskitrs of Peking and then had withdrawn, and concerning the opinion question, Admiral Elliot wrote:

> I have seen (I suppose Newspaper) remarks on the impropriety of not forcing the negotiations in the North when we were once there. In the first place, it was *simply impossible*. The anchorage off the Piho is quite open—the cold and foul-weather monsoon was just setting in—our communication with the shore had already become difficult and doubtful, and would very shortly cease entirely, and the coast would be frozen. Even had it been otherwise, our demands for satisfaction were *for what had occurred at Canton*, and had assuredly never been faithfully reported to Pekin; constant reference would therefore have been necessary to Canton, and an answer could not be expected in less than *three months*—the ordinary post being forty-five days. But it is useless to combat the remarks of people who are perfectly ignorant, not only of the main points, but of all local circumstances, which often have great weight. For instance, the Chinese opium trade is talked of in England as if it was carried on *by English smuggling vessels*, in defiance of the Chinese custom-house authorities, whereas it is as open a trade as any other. Opium is prohibited by Imperial decree, but every year a duty is fixed on it, and agreed to, *by the importers and the Mandarins,*

all of which is shared between the Governor of the province and the Mandarins of various sorts.

The opium vessels lay at the islands called by the Chinese the '*Outer Waters*,' which is beyond the control of Chinese customhouse officers, and there the Chinese *opium boats* come for what they want, paying on the spot in dollars. . . . They go up the rivers openly, passing close to the Chinese forts, where occasionally they are called in and the opium chests counted, I suppose as a check on their cheating the Mandarins of the settled duty; the Chinese pay the duty, the ship importing it has nothing to do with that. The trade is as open as any other, and, in fact, the importing ships have nothing to do with even *the authorized smuggling*, if such a term can be applied to it, merely because the government does not receive the duty levied by their own officers and paid in the same way any other duty is paid.

If we were to prohibit the opium trade with China there would not be one chest less imported. It is a profitable trade, and Foreigners would carry it on; and if you prohibit the growth of opium or its export *in India*, Java alone could with ease supply all China—they already grow a great deal, and could grow any quantity the market required.[5e] . . . for all nations carry on the opium trade. I have myself seen Dutch, American, Swedish and Danish opium vessels, and there is a considerable Spanish and Portuguese trade carried on.[5e]

The concern of Russia and France towards British interests and activities in the Far East is engaging. Palmerston, in a despatch to the two Elliots, dated Foreign Office, 13th January 1841,[3c] reported and enclosed a despatch [3d] from the Marquis of Clauricarde, Her Majesty's Ambassador at the Court of St. Petersburg, that Russia was fretting over Britain's objects in China. Palmerston related that the last session of Parliament announced

. . . redress of injuries inflicted upon British subjects by the Chinese authorities, satisfaction for the affront offered to the British Crown, and security for the future for the persons and property of British Subjects trading to China,[3e]

were, still, the British objectives in China.

Several days later, Palmerston informed the two Elliots [3f] that he had just received a despatch from Her Majesty's chargé d'affaires at Rio de Janeiro, M. Onseley, that it was supposed there that a squadron of the largest vessels of war belonging to the French squadron in the River Plate was about to proceed immediately to China. Palmerston, in his despatch to the Elliots, included a list [3g] of these French war vessels, which list he had taken from Onseley's despatch to the Foreign Office of 16th October 1840, and, also, an extract from Onseley's despatch, dated Rio de Janeiro, 26th November 1840, which informed the Viscount Palmerston that

. . . I fear that six (?) of the larger vessels of War from the French Squadron in the River Plate are to proceed immediately to China, there to form a squadron of observation.

Some rumour is afloat that this detachment of the Squadron is to take possession of some Island or Territory on the Coast of China.[3h]

Returning to war and negotiation, it is remembered that Lin Tse-su's policy had been to crush the British. As results of this policy, the British force had come very close to Peking and Lin had been banished to Sinkiang. Kishen had realized and advocated to the Emperor the impolicy of Lin's course and had represented that, while the aggressive acts of the barbarian English must be checked by force, the demands to be made upon them must be supported by negotiations—that only by negotiations could the opium traffic be suppressed. The Emperor, provoked by Lin's failure, sent Kishen south to Canton as High Commissioner to adopt, in the Chinese approved and time-tested method of wearying their opponents by procrastination, a policy of conciliation. But, at Canton, Kishen had not only his English opponent to deal with but the Chinese war party, friends of the irreconcilable Lin, impatient with the harm done their coffers by the events of the past months. On his side, Captain Elliot, though during the past year having shown himself inclined to measures which might lead to peaceful solution, was still unwavering in his adherence to the irreducible minimum—a base for British operations, always Hong Kong in Elliot's mind. Surely the British deserved a place to fly their flag in as much peace as did the Portuguese at Macao.

In these respective attitudes, Elliot, all through December of 1840, put the British case to Kishen who, knowing that the cession of national territory would never be forgiven by the Emperor, received the case and, from day to day, postponed definite reply. On 5th January 1841, Elliot was writing Palmerston of his hopes that, by patience and tact, the Commissioner would have been disposed 'more readily to concede conditions necessary for placing our future trade and intercourse upon a secure footing; an object which is no doubt the chief purpose of Her Majesty's Government in despatching forces to these shores.' [2b] Yet, Elliot continued, the Emperor was inclined only 'to force us back to Canton upon the old system' [2b] which Elliot reminded Palmerston would be 'a settlement . . . at once incompatible with your Lordship's Instructions, and with the possibility of maintaining any honourable or secure footing for the foreign trade in this Empire.' [2b] Elliot continued his report to Palmerston:

. . . But resolved to admit of no relaxation as respects the future, I venture to express the belief that the reasonable and yielding spirit of the Chinese minister as far as it has gone will be my justification for having manifested a disposition to mitigate his difficulties concerning the past, greatly beyond the letter of my Instructions. And I hope too it will be a satisfactory reflection and negociations have been interrupted upon the material consideration of future security and improvement, rather than upon the inadequacy of indemnity, or upon any point having reference to the past.[2b]

By early January 1841, Elliot realized that only by using the force at his disposal could the Chinese be brought to terms. Believing the seizure of the two forts at the mouth of the Bogue, Chuenpee on the east and Tycocktow on the west, to be the effective blow required, for the Chinese were highly sensitive about the gate to Canton, Elliot, early for 7th January 1841, ordered attack. Accordingly, line-of-battle ships with frigates, steamers, and transports moved in and, in a sixty-minute engagement in which 500 Chinese were killed and 300 wounded, the two batteries at Chuenpee and Tycocktow were taken. During the operations, Elliot himself was on board the *Nemesis*, the East India Company's iron war-steamer which distinguished herself by a conspicuous attack on the enemy's forts and the annihilation of 11 powerful war-junks, the flower of the Celestial Navy.[XIV] The British suffered no fatal casualties and, now, the fleet stood free to enter the Bogue, capture the two inner forts and that on Tiger Island, and sail on to Canton itself. But Elliot, believing that Kishen might have had enough, called off the action for that day. On the next, 8th January, as his forces were preparing to advance to attack the Bogue forts, Elliot received a request to meet Kishen that day at Anunghoi. The meeting was held, an armistice was agreed upon, and negotiations were resumed. By 20th January, an agreement called the Convention of Chuenpee had been drawn up and signed by Elliot and Kishen, acting as Plenipotentiaries for Britain and China. The Convention's terms were, in British fashion this time, elegantly concise: cession of Hong Kong to the British Crown, an indemnity of six million dollars by annual instalments of a million, official intercourse to be on an equal footing, trade to be reopened at Canton and carried on there until Hong Kong was ready. Much later, Elliot expressed his personal opinion that the Emperor at Peking, upon learning the terms, was convinced that Elliot, to secure such favourable terms, had bribed Kishen.[2s]

In his despatch to Palmerston, dated at Macao, 21st January 1841, Elliot informed the Foreign Office that

> Efficient protection, a quiet improvement of opportunities, and the most liberal and equal privileges to foreigners and English people at the new settlement Hong Kong will, I believe, rapidly draw the whole foreign commerce with this Empire under our own Flag. . . .[2d]

XIV In March 1840 the *Nemesis* sailed from Portsmouth for the East Indies, attracting much attention as the first iron steamer to endeavour to double the Cape of Good Hope; she encountered terrific gales and was split amidships on both sides.

Regarding the selection of Hong Kong, Elliot continued that he was convinced

> ... that there is not a nobler Harbour nor a more valuable position in every point of view, in the Queen's Possessions.[2e] ... Her Majesty's protection and influence will make it within a very few years, one of the most important, and perhaps the most interesting Possession of the British Crown.[2f]

As to his instructions, Elliot wrote Palmerston that, in his decisions, he had been guided by 'points where I may consider it necessary for the public interests to regard the general spirit and purposes of the Instructions rather than their letter.'[2g] And that

> They (Britain's officers in China) have thought that whilst there was a hope of indemnity for the past, and security for the future by peaceful means, it was their bounden duty upon every motive of humanity and comprehensive policy to refrain from casting, upon Her Majesty's Arms the stain of a calamitous character of warfare against a Government and people wholly unable to contend against our prowess.[2g]

Furthermore, Elliot stated publicly what was to become known as the Open Door and about which so much was to be heard in future years:

> Her Majesty's government has sought for no special privilege in China exclusively for the advantage of British subjects and merchants, and he is only performing his duty in offering the protection of the British Flag to the subjects and citizens and ships of foreign Powers that may resort to Her Majesty's Possession.[3i]

Even the traders in China, apparently, had no criticisms on this occasion of the Convention of Chuenpee. They, still led by Matheson, who had always called Elliot too mild and hesitating, now expatiated on the advantages of Hong Kong and expressed confidence in the future. The cession of Hong Kong meant that the whole foreign commerce of China would be under the British flag. That there was no mention about the drug traffic in the Convention was highly gratifying. Opium could be stored at Hong Kong without contravening the treaty and distributed from that port with much decorum.

Kishen, too, was pleased with his accomplishments. He felt that, with the cession of Hong Kong, a barren rock far to the south, the Emperor would be gratified for the evacuation of Ting-hai, a large town halfway to the capital and from which Nanking, the second city of China, could be threatened and the vast trade of the Yangtze blocked with ease. Kishen had saved his own and China's face: he had cheated the barbarians and driven them into the China Seas. As for the six million indemnity, he could wring that from the Hong merchants.

But both Plenipotentiaries, British and Chinese, soon were to feel the wrath of their respective governments. Palmerston's crushing letter to Elliot is dated 21st April 1841. Since his dressing down in Commons for not sending Elliot precise and ample instructions and, regardless of his sarcastic answers to Commons that it was both impracticable and impossible to instruct a man thousands of miles away, Palmerston had addressed lengthy and infeasible epistles to China.[3j] On 3rd February 1841, Palmerston, writing the Elliots, stated that the Foreign Office desired adherence to the instructions of 20th February 1840 (at pp. 28-30) and favoured, contrary to Charles Elliot and to the Governor-General of India, in place of Hong Kong, the selection of an insular station 'somewhere on the Eastern Coast, and either in the Chusan group, or not far from it' (at p. 30).

Palmerston stated that such a selection

> . . . would afford to British Trade an opening to the wealthy and populous Countries and Cities on the central part of the Eastern Coast of China, and would, by means of the Great Canal and of the large Rivers whose mouths lie in that quarter, give to British commodities an easy channel of access to the interior of the Chinese Empire. Therefore, although it might be convenient to have also some secure station at the mouth of the Canton River, the main point to be gained is a position off the East Coast (at p. 30).

Then, in a despatch dated 4th February 1841, the Foreign Secretary itemized for the two Plenipotentiaries the compensation to be demanded of the Chinese Government.[3k] Perhaps a bit presumptuously, Palmerston had, on 3rd February, informed the Lords Court of the Admiralty that 'it has been stated to me by a person well acquainted with China' (at p. 40) that 'at the proper season it would not be difficult for a British Force to ascend the Peiko (sic) River to the point where it is intersected by the Great Canal and take possession of a town at that intersection and, thus, cut off Pekin (sic) from supplies' from 'that Town' (at pp. 40-41).[3l] Palmerston asked that such information be conveyed to Admiral Elliot, commanding the Expedition in the China Seas.

Several weeks later, Palmerston wrote the two Elliots:

> . . . Her Majesty's Government having taken into their consideration the circumstances connected with the China Opium Trade, I have to instruct you to endeavor to make some arrangement with the Chinese Government for the admission of opium into China, as an article of lawful commerce.[3m]

But Elliot, inured, for several years past, to meagre instructions, to depending upon his own judgment in emergencies and, in truth, to the subsequent approval that Palmerston invariably had accorded his actions, had carried out his instructions as he deemed expedient in the circumstances as they unfolded. As sole Plenipotentiary, he assumed that he possessed discretion; but Palmerston now wrote otherwise. The Foreign Secretary's disavowal of Elliot's action no doubt expressed the feeling in Parliament and in the country. Even though the war, one mixed up with opium traffic indeed, had been begun slowly and with misgivings, the people, flushed by the exploits of their army and navy, wanted victory— and trade! When the actual terms of the Chuenpee Convention were made known, Lord Melbourne, the Prime Minister, stated in the House of Lords that instructions had been sent to Captain Elliot in China that, if a treaty based on the preliminary articles of Chuenpee had been made, it would not be ratified by Her Majesty's Government.[10b] The young Victoria, in righteous indignation, expressed this same feeling when, on 13th April, she wrote to the King of the Belgians:

> The Chinese business vexes us much, and Palmerston is deeply mortified at it. *All* we wanted might have been got, if it had not been for the unaccountably strange conduct of Charles Elliot . . . who completely disobeyed his instructions and *tried* to get the *lowest* terms he could.[24y]

At a Cabinet meeting, held 30th April, it was decided that the government could not sanction any treaty based on the preliminary agreement, the Convention of Chuenpee, and that agreement was repudiated; Sir Henry Pottinger was sent out to relieve Elliot, get a larger indemnity, reoccupy Ting-hai, and demand trading ports.[24y] Elliot, the following August, was to receive, in Palmerston's despatch which was delivered by Pottinger upon his arrival in China, the news of his political shipwreck. On 3rd May 1841, Palmerston, writing to Bremer and Elliot,[xv, 3n] said:

> . . . It will not be necessary for Captain Elliot to accompany the Force to Chusan; because no negotiation is to be commenced until the arrival of the new Plenipotentiary whom Her Majesty's Government intend to send out by the next monthly occasion; and as the arrival of that Plenipotentiary will set Captain Elliot free, and enable him to proceed at once on his return to England, he will be better placed for that purpose in the neighbourhood of Canton, than he would be at Chusan.[30]

Palmerston concluded this despatch by saying that the new plenipotentiary would carry with him full instructions for his future proceedings (at p. 53), that it was 'not considered necessary to associate any other Person with him, and (that) the negotiations will be entrusted to him singly' (at p. 53). Furthermore,

---

xv Upon receipt, March 1841, of the information of Admiral Elliot's poor health, Palmerston authorized Captain Charles Elliot and Commodore Sir James John Gordon Bremer as Her Majesty's Plenipotentiaries to China.

. . . it is sufficient for me on the present occasion to say that Her Majesty's Government are not satisfied with the arrangements made by Captain Elliot as reported in his Dispatches to No. 5 of the 21st Of January 1841, the last at present received; and that it does not appear to Her Majesty's Government that Captain Elliot had any sufficient reason for having departed as he has done from the Instructions which he had received.[3p]

Meanwhile, at so great a distance, English policy in China remained under Captain Elliot's control until the following August, when the despatches from England arrived. However, that the Convention of Chuenpee was null and void he soon learned from his opponents. Shortly after the Convention was signed and sent to the Emperor, Kishen received the Dragon's reply. The Son of Heaven was finished with the increasing insolence and violence of the English barbarians; their rebel leader (Elliot) should be brought to Peking and punished; Kishen, succumbing to the wiles of the rebel barbarians, had even signed away Imperial Territory of the Celestial Empire (Hong Kong); for such high misdemeanour, Kishen was deprived of his post and ordered to leave Canton in chains for Peking. There, the luckless Grand Secretary was tried, condemned to death, and his property confiscated. Yet, perhaps Kishen's immodest fortune salved the Dragon; for he was not executed but exiled, as Lin had been to Ili, to the frozen frontier of the Amur River.

The remainder of Elliot's story in China can be related as epilogue. The Convention of Chuenpee of 20th January 1841,[2h] being repudiated by the Emperor in February, preparations to renew hostilities were observed by Elliot who, to anticipate them, renewed hostilities on 23rd February, broke through the Bogue batteries on 26th February, and, on 2nd March, brought his ships up to Whampoa.[2i] Another truce was made, trade was reopened, and the season's tea quickly shipped.[2i] But the Chinese, throughout April, continued their preparations to attack and the air, elsewhere than at Canton, was filled with talk of all-out war. Captain Elliot allowed time for the season's trade to be finished and, then, alarmed at the growing reports of 'aggressive preparation' at Canton and 'particularly the rearmament of the Fort in the Western Suburb, contrary to express understanding'[2j] he demanded the immediate cessation of hostile preparations. The Chinese evaded answer and on 17th May Elliot moved up the military and naval forces. The following day, 18th May, in a *Circular to Merchants*, Elliot ordered all merchants at Canton 'to withdraw from Canton for safety.' [2k] On the 21st, when the forces were within ten miles of Canton, he ordered all foreign residents to leave the city before sunset.[2l] That same night, the Chinese fire-rafts opened fire on the British ships and the Chinese soldiery and mob plundered the evacuated factories. Elliot's proclamation, dated 22nd

May 1841, to the People of Canton declared that he was sparing Canton and the whole province 'in recollection of the long and peaceful intercourse which has subsisted between them and the Western Nations.' [2m] On the 27th, when Elliot was ready to counter by an assault, with 2,395 men and artillery, on Canton itself, the Chinese faltered and ransomed the city by paying six million dollars. The British forces then withdrew outside the Bogue.

Elliot, wisely, had decided against occupying Canton, where he feared his small force would either be swallowed up in the dark streets or become unruly with drink and loot. Concerning the ransom, Elliot wrote Palmerston that 'the city of Canton has been spared from misery and desolation, which nothing but our own forbearance could have averted' and that 'it was very gratifying to be able to inform your Lordship' that the settlement had afforded the British 'the time to get rid of the immense mass of shipping and goods then lying off these coasts, and to send home about 28 millions of Tea.' [2n] Availing himself of the July mail from Bengal to England, Elliot, in a despatch dated at Canton, 12th April 1841, had told Palmerston:

> . . . The City and trade of Canton and the whole Province are flourishing, at the date of this despatch, under the protection of the British Flag, and the people perfectly understand they would be subject to a recurrence of renewed oppression by their own Government, and that the whole would languish, from the very hour that our protection was withdrawn.[2o]

Several weeks later, Elliot, writing to Auckland, expressed 'his great satisfaction' that Auckland 'deemed it wise and right to spare the city of Canton.' [2p]

Meanwhile, though the ceding of Hong Kong had been cancelled, the British, during the early spring of 1841, had been settling there, proceeding to lay out the new city, and to organize a colonial government whose attention was carefully directed to the propulsion of trade at Hong Kong.[2q] On 7th June, Captain Elliot issued a proclamation declaring to the

> . . . merchants and traders of Canton and all parts of the empire, that they and their ships have free permission to resort to and trade at the port of Hongkong, where they will receive full protection from the high officers of the British nation; and, Hongkong being on the shores of the Chinese empire, neither will there be any charges on imports and exports payable to the British government.[24z]

After thus declaring Hong Kong a free port, and writing Palmerston that he trusted Her Majesty's Government would follow up with promotion 'the brilliant conduct of Her Majesty's Forces in the late operations in this country,' [2t] —where, due to 'difficult navigation in waters little known' and to the 'much more fatal calamity of extensive sickness,' the forces had suffered extensively [25]—Elliot seems to have been at a loss as to what to do next. On 7th July 1841, he informed Palmerston that he had just learned of the 'censure upon my public conduct' and that he was 'quite ready to attempt the justification of my own conduct' when 'I am called upon to do so by competent authority.[21] He had taken no further action when his successor, Sir Henry Pottinger, arrived on 10th August. [24z]

On Elliot's immediate departure for home, Pottinger, equipped with Lord Palmerston's instructions which made him Sole Plenipotentiary and Chief Superintendent of Trade, with power to decide on every point connected with the negotiations,[24z] set out to recapture Ting-hai and to make demands for a final settlement of all outstanding Anglo-Chinese questions.[19a] On 21st August 1841, he started north; en route, on the 26th, he took Amoy; then, Ting-hai on 1st October and he proceeded to seize certain other cities in the vicinity to secure his position. In January 1842, Pottinger returned south and resumed the organization of the tea trade at Hong Kong so that the seasonal shipments could be made. Meanwhile, at home, Palmerston had given way to Aberdeen, the Foreign Secretary of the Peel Administration, and the new government's determined attitude is noted in Aberdeen's despatch to Pottinger when he wrote:

> . . . Although success may have attended her Majesty's Arms, it is by no means probable that the War should have been brought to a termination; and in this state of uncertainty therefore, Her Majesty's Government have determined to make the necessary preparations for carrying on the ensuing campaign with vigour, and with effect.[3q]

To enable him to finish the war before the next season began, London doubled Pottinger's troops by a reinforcement that brought his numbers to 10,000; and they instructed him to move against and take the strategic second capital, Nanking, which is situated on the Yangtze just north of Ting-hai, rather than to try again at the Peiho's mouth. When all the tea had been shipped home, Pottinger, in May 1842, moved north in a course of victory and, on 14th August, the Chinese agreed to the British demands[24za] and, on 29th August 1843, the Treaty of Nanking was signed.[24zb] By this dictated peace, and a supplementary agreement signed near Canton, in October 1843, the British, at long last, secured all that they had been wanting since the Macartney Mission in the 18th century. The provisions flowed from a pen held by the British mercantilists. Hong Kong was ceded to the Crown; five ports, afterwards called the Treaty Ports, in a line up the China coast were opened—Canton, Amoy, Foochow, Ningpo, and Shanghai—where the British merchants and their families could reside permanently, having their own Consuls and courts, with the right to import

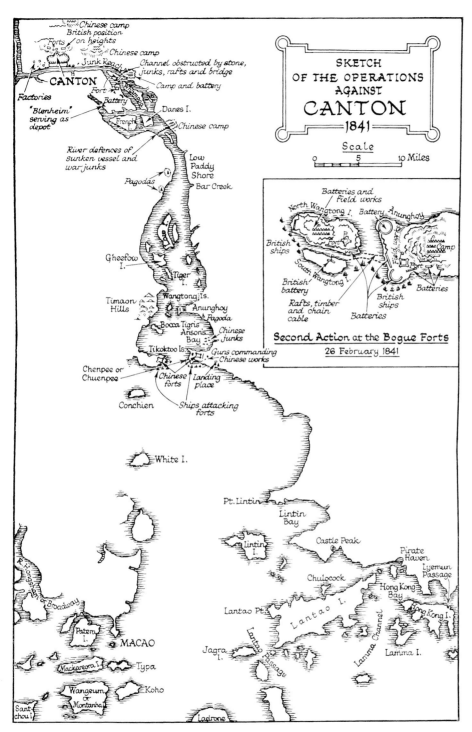

Sketch of the operations against Canton
(from the map by James Wyld. London: 1841)

Top   Houqua (Hunter, William C., *The 'Fan Kwae' at Canton Before Treaty Days,*
1825–1844. London: Kegan Paul, Trench & Co., 1882).

Centre left   The heir apparent.   *Centre right*   Macao egg-boat.

Bottom   Chin-Tchew junk (Downing, C. Toogood, *The Fan-Qui in China in 1836–7,*
I, II, III. London: Henry Colburn, 1838).

under a fixed customs tariff and without the necessity of buying and selling through the Hong merchants; and the Chinese were to pay 6,000,000 dollars for the 20,000 seized chests—in the treaty, this sum was described as indemnity for property forcibly surrendered as ransom for the lives of British subjects, *not* as money compensating smugglers for the loss of contraband! Lastly, China had to pay 15,000,000 dollars to cover the cost of the Pottinger expedition and outstanding debts. Thus was China 'persuaded,' in 1842, to abandon her policy of seclusion and emerge into the modern world 'brotherhood' of trading states. And, interestingly enough, the Treaty said nothing about the very subject which had caused the first Anglo-Chinese War, but 'it was hoped smuggling would cease.' As a matter of record, the British did not undertake to stop the traffic, even though it was pointed out in Commons that illegal commerce could have been overcome by getting the Indian Government to reduce poppy cultivation and by prohibiting the export of the prepared drug. Though, by September 1842, Palmerston and the Whigs had gone out and the Tories under Peel had come in, the new Cabinet feared, in spite of the anti-opium speeches of some of its supporters on the 1840 vote of censure, to endanger the stability of the Indian revenues by so drastic a blow as one directed at the drug trade. And the merchants, on their part, with the added facilities of five Treaty Ports, and an emporium at Hong Kong, increased their trade volume enormously and the opium traffic thrived until 1908.[242b]

Charles Elliot and his small family returned home, where he sought to justify to the new Conservative Cabinet his definite policy, ever since he had, in December 1836, assumed the position of Superintendent, of quiet penetration in China—this policy he had tried, in spite of the warlike events of 1839, to maintain. Elliot, with his eyes on the past, had wanted to improve the position and trading interests of the British representative and British trade at Canton. Later, with his eyes on the future, he had stressed the cession of Hong Kong and the securing for the British all and the same privileges which might be granted to any other foreign power. The length of the coast up to the Yangtze and the extension of British trade to the north were not so basic to Elliot as that of compelling the Cantonese to remain quiet, certainly between March and May, so that the British traders could export the tea. Elliot, insufficiently instructed, stationed in a faraway outpost, and militarily dependent on the Governor-General of India, sought to gain by diplomacy all that he could and not to engage in unnecessary or long hostilities. Palmerston, at first so negligent in his instructions to his agents in China, came, after his dressing down

59

in Commons, to be ready for the use of force in order to settle the future relations of Great Britain and China. Palmerston, too, was in close touch with home opinion, largely mercantile; Elliot, like his predecessors, was not in sympathy with a large group of the trading community in China, certainly not those who regarded the honest objectors to the opium traffic as 'those Saints in England.' On her part, China claimed a monopoly of civilization, to her all westerners were barbarians—fan-quis, foreign devils, wanderers, outlandish demons—differing only in turbulence and martial ability from such of her tributary potentates as those of Siam or the Loochow Islands. The Emperor, as the Son of Heaven, was the earth-dwelling mediator between the Almighty and all creatures below. As such George III or Victoria was the same as any other dependent ruler—with this exception, perhaps—the British Barbarians in the Celestial Empire were the most arrogant foreign devils that had ever gotten into the Empire. These opinions were regarded by the British as a mark of Oriental stupidity and it was this chasm of difference in attitude towards each other that made impossible the harmonious development of international relations between China and Great Britain—by the beginning of the 19th century, incomparably the most important Western State in the China Seas and, by 1815, flushed with victory over Napoleon.

Elliot, realizing all these considerations, wrote a memorandum to Aberdeen reviewing his conduct. This document was circulated to the members of the new Conservative Cabinet.[27f] He justified his taking over the opium in 1839 by quoting the Duke of Wellington's approval of that act. He thought he had acted wisely in not blockading the Canton River, when he moved up to the Peiho, because the Chinese knew that the trade was more important to the foreigners than to themselves and to have stopped it would have been doing their work. It was not necessary, for proper prosecution of the war, to neglect commercial interests. His policy had resulted, 1839-41, in a clearance of 50,000 tons of British shipping and a trade to the value of ten million pounds sterling.

Continuing his own justification, Elliot said that, after Chusan Island had been occupied, he had not enough ships both to blockade the Yangtze and to go to the Peiho. Admiral Elliot had overruled him in his desire to concentrate on the Yangtze and to negotiate there. Subsequently, at the Peiho, the two Plenipotentiaries were unable to effect any military pressure and, there, Kishen, as his subsequent punishment proved, had not meant to deceive the British but had seriously overestimated the strength of the peace party in Peking. By November 1840, when he had returned to Canton, Elliot had, owing to death and disease at Chusan, only 2,500 effectives and it was this diminution of his force that seemed to fall within his instructions —'circumstances may happen and questions may arise, which have not been foreseen by Her Majesty's government, in such case you will use your discretion, guiding yourself according to the spirit of your instructions.' He was of opinion that he had secured everything essential except the money payments for the expedition. With regard to the debts owed by the Hong merchants to the British, Elliot, in June 1841, had informed the Governor-General that the two parties concerned had come to an agreement which was being carried out. The Hong system would die a natural death, Elliot was certain, if the right which he had acquired for individual Chinese to trade with the British at Hong Kong had been maintained. Yet, the question was solving itself, and the Hong merchants were but little more than brokers. Elliot defended his arrangement whereby a committee of British and Hong merchants was to settle the terms of a commercial treaty, as these Chinese merchants were very much under the influence of the more powerful British. Further, he contended that to secure additional authorized ports of trade, while the opium question remained unsettled, was to place so many more hostages in the power of the Chinese. Chusan, with its unhealthy climate and hostile peasantry, was not as good a settlement as Hong Kong; and it was a mistake to suppose that Hong Kong would be a British Macao. As to the criticism that he cared too much for the Chinese, Elliot said that he cared more for lasting British honour and substantial British interests to protect a helpless and friendly people—a people who loved both their country and their profit. Elliot continued that England might well do better by a course of continuing to enlist Chinese profit rather than a course of raising up Chinese love of their country against England. In conclusion, Elliot wrote Lord Aberdeen that he thought, given time to explain more fully his motives between 7th January 1841, and the resumption of hostilities in May, he could have satisfied Palmerston.[27f]

It appears certain that, contrary to his underlying hopes and policy, when relieved, in August 1841, Elliot was about to do what Pottinger was equipped, both by instructions and forces, to do and did—to blockade the Yangtze. There is little doubt that there, on the Yangtze, Elliot might have won the very terms which were secured at Nanking in 1842. But, as his own words expressed his policy in China, Elliot had sensed that

... Force was requisite, but forbearance was indispensable.[2u]

CHARLES ELLIOT R.N.

BIBLIOGRAPHY & REFERENCES

MICROFILM

1 F.O.R. 228/3, 1836. To Foreign Office. Captain Elliot, R.N.
   a p.222; b p.235; c p.248; d p.227; e p.229.

2 F.O.R. 228/15, 1841. To Foreign Office. Captain Elliot, R.N.
   a pp.71,73,75,268,271,273-77,349-51,391-95,407-9,411-21; b p.5; c pp.385-88; d p.128 e p.133; f p.134;
   g p.132; h p.193ff; i p.239; j p.354; k p.367; l p.369; m p.373; n p.349; o p.287; p p.435; q p.352; r p.378;
   s p.384; t p.428; u pp.226-28.

3 F.O.R. 228/17, 1841. From Foreign Office to Sir H. Pottinger, R. A. Elliot and Captain Elliot.
   a pp.159-67; b p.11; c p.14; d p.15; e p.17; f p.19; g p.21; h p.20; i p.47; j pp.23-30; k p.37; l p.40;
   m pp.42-45; n p.46; o pp.50-53; p p.53; q pp.193-201.

4 British Parliamentary Papers, 1840; XXXVI, No. 6.

OTHER AND PRINTED MATERIALS

5 Elliot, Sir George, *Memoir of Admiral The Honourable Sir George Elliot, Written for His Children*,
   London: H. Weede, Printer, 1863.
   a pp.133-35; b pp.136-38; c pp.138-41; d p.141; e pp.147-49; f p.149; g p.135.

6 Letters (1950–51): W. G. Beasley, Professor, School of Oriental and African Studies, The University
   of London, to Clagette Blake.

7 Letters (1950–51): Maurice Collis to Clagette Blake.

8 Letters (1950–51): W. J. Keswick to Clagette Blake.

9 Letters (1949–51): W. N. Medlicott, Professor, The University of Exeter, to Clagette Blake.

10 Hansard, *Parliamentary Debates*, 3rd Ser., Vols. XVIII (1833), XIX (1833), XX (1833), LIII (1840).
   LVII (1841). London: Thomas Curson Hansard.
   a LIII, cols. 669-836, pp.845-955; b LVII, p.1491.

11 Loines, Elma (ed.), 'More Canton letters of Abiel Abbot Low, William Hanry Low, and Edward
   Low (1837–1844)', *The Essex Institute Historical Collections*, Vol. LXXXV, No. 3. Salem, Massachusetts, July 1949.

12 Maps. Division of Maps, The Library of Congress.

13 *The Great Britain Public Record Office Lists and Indexes* 52. London: His Majesty's Stationery Office,
   1929.

14 Beasley, W. G., *Great Britain and the Opening of Japan*, 1834–50. Unpublished doctoral thesis, School
   of Oriental and African Studies, The University of London, 1950.

15 *China Year Book for 1916*.

16 Collis, Maurice, *Foreign Mud*. New York: Alfred A. Knopf, 1947. (This gives a skilful and delightful
   account of the international opium trade.)

17 Downing, C. Toogood, *The Fan-Qui in China in* 1836-7. 3 vols., illustrated. London: Henry Colburn,
   Publisher, 1838. Loaned by the University of Washington.

18 Downing, C. Toogood, *The Stranger in China; or, The Fan-Qui's Visit to the Celestial Empire, in*
   1836-7. 2 vols. Philadelphia: Lea and Blanchard, Publishers, 1838. Microfilmed by permission of
   The University of Washington.
   a II, ch. x; b II, p.142; c II, pp.142-45.

19 Eames, James Bromley, *The English in China*. London: Sir Isaac Pitman and Sons Ltd., 1909.
   a p.490.

20 *Edinburgh Review*, LXVIII (October 1838). Edinburgh: A. Constable, 1838.
   a pp.46-75.

21 Fairbank, John King, *The United States and China* in *The American Foreign Policy Library*, ed. Charles
   Sumner. Cambridge: Harvard University Press, 1948.

22 Hunter, William C., *Bits of Old China*. London: Keagan Paul, Trench and Company, 1885. Microfilmed by permission of Standford University Library.

23 Hunter, William C., *The 'Fan Kwae' at Canton Before Treaty Days*, 1825–1844. London: Keagan Paul,
   Trench and Company, 1882. Microfilmed by permission of Yale College Library.

24 Morse, Hosea Ballou, *The International Relations of the Chinese Empire*, Vol. I. 3 vols. London:
   Longmans, Green and Company, 1910. (Morse's principal sources were: (1) *Correspondence and*

Papers Relating to China, a White Paper, laid before Parliament in 1840, containing all the British Government's instructions to its various representatives at Canton, despatches that passed between the Government and its representatives, and the Parliamentary Report on the enquiry into the seizure of the opium by Lin in 1839; (2) *The Chinese Repository*, a quarterly paper published, not by the mercantile group but by Protestant missionaries, in Canton and Macao during the currency of the 1830s.)

a p.152; *b* p.157; *c* pp.213-19; *d* p.219; *e* p.199; *f* p.224; *g* p.229; *h* p.231; *i* p.232; *j* p.237; *k* p.253; *l* p.244; *m* p.245; *n* p.246; *o* p.257; *p* p.255; *q* p.260; *r* p.262; *s* p.261; *t* p.263; *u* p.xxxiv; *v* p.265; *w* p.266; *x* p.267; *y* p.272; *z* p.287; *za* pp.288-96; *zb* pp.298-318.

25 Philips, C. H., *The East India Company*, 1784–1834. Manchester: Manchester University Press, 1940.

26 *Quarterly Review*, LVI (July 1836). London: J. Murray, 1836.
   a pp. 436-37.

27 Costin, *Great Britain and China*, 1833–60.
   a p.67; *b* p.62; *c* p.77; *d* p.74; *e* p.75; *f* pp.93-96.

28 O'Byrne, *Naval Biographical Dictionary*.
   a p.1085; *b* p.533.

V

Elliot in the New World
The Texas Mission

———————❦❦❦❦———————

THE Texas question, both recognition and annexation, was for a decade a subject of national mania and world importance. On 4th August, 1841, Elliot had been appointed as chargé d'affaires to the Republic by the Melbourne Government, although, both for government and personal reasons, it was the summer of 1842 before he went to Texas.[4a] Four years earlier, near midnight on 3rd March, 1837, President Andrew Jackson's last official act had been to consummate the ardent work of the Texan commissioners to Washington-on-the-Potomac by appointing a Louisianian, Alcée La Branche, chargé d'affaires of the Republic of Texas. Thus did the United States recognize the Republic and end the first phase of the movement for annexation to the United States. And thus did the United States officially forge another link in a long chain of events that one day, almost a decade later, would result in the Mexican war. That same night, in March 1837, the President and his guests, the Texan commissioners, rejoiced and toasted in wine the launching of the infant Republic.[48a] Later, one of the Texans to Washington reported that President Jackson, in order to paralyse the opposition of the North and East to annexation, privately encouraged the Texans to expand their boundaries to the Pacific Ocean.[62a]

France, October 1839-January 1840, was the first European nation to recognize Texan independence [47a] and Holland, January-June 1841, the second.[XVI, 47b, 48b, 57a] In September 1841, success in Central America came to Texas when she formulated a quasi-treaty with Yucatan.[48c,d, 66a, 68a] Belgium, though anxious for commercial benefits resulting from a ready market in Texas, and Texas, anxious for Belgian loans as well as commercial

xvi The velvet-bound copy of the Texas-Holland treaty, in both English and Dutch, and signed by King Willem, is in The State Archives, Austin.

64

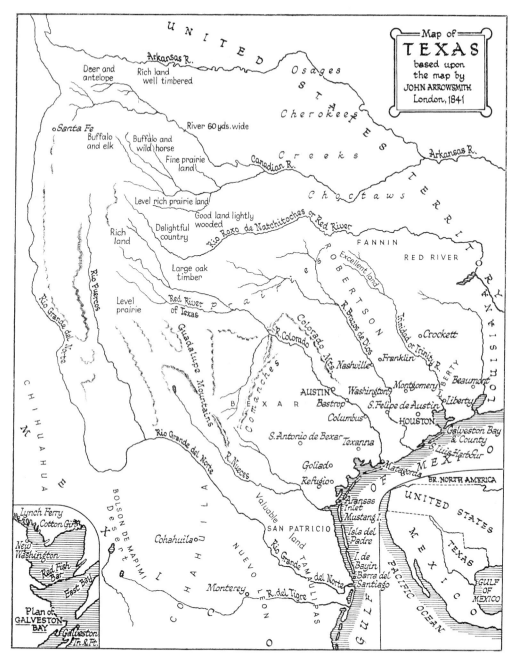

Map of Texas (Kennedy, William. *Texas: The Rise, Progress and Prospects of the Republic of Texas*, I. London: 1841)

benefits, negotiated fruitlessly from 1839 to 1844.[48e, 57b, 65a, 80a] On 17th April 1844, a treaty of friendship, commerce, and navigation between Texas and the Hanseatic Republics of Lubeck, Bremen, and Hamburgh was signed.[48f, 65b] An engaging stipulation to this treaty provided that, in view of the close national and political connection existing between the three Hanseatic Republics and the other States of the German Confederation, the treaty might be extended to any of the various States of the German Confederation which desired to join. In November 1840, England and Texas, after long and tedious negotiations, had agreed upon three treaties: one provided that Great Britain would act as mediator between Texas and Mexico and, should English mediation result in a treaty within six months after it was offered to the Mexican government, Texas was to assume one million pounds sterling of the Mexican foreign debt; the other two treaties provided for recognition of independence, regulation of commerce, and suppression of the slave trade.[46a, 78a] But in spite of the Republic's successes in the United States, Central America, and Europe, she failed to secure recognition in Mexico which regarded Texas as its truant province, which it was.

Apparently, the entrance of Texas on to the world stage was 'a matter of the gravest importance.' To any nation recognizing the infant Republic, and most certainly to any nation establishing connections with it, various and perplexing problems would surely come. Both Mexico and the United States would see to that. Opportunity to acquire great influence in America 'by dealing skilfully with Texas' waited as award for any nation willing to risk the dangerous complications involved.

> The essential alternatives presented to the United States were either to acquire Texas, or to risk the possibility of its becoming a dangerous instrument of European powers. But the worst feature of the case, for England and for the United States in particular, was that in any attempt to settle upon a policy the irritating question of slavery always thrust itself forward.[67a]

'Throughout the period of Texas independence American statesmen were uneasy about British designs in Texas'[59a] and this fear was especially evident between the years 1840 and 1846. As early as May 1836, in a United States Senate debate, warnings against Britain's interests and plans for Texas were voiced. The Senators were considering recognition and the North's Daniel Webster, convinced that a 'European power' sought to entice Texas and might injure United States' interests there, declared that Texas ought to be recognized as soon as the American government had official information that Texas was independent and possessed resources adequate to maintain independence. The South's John C. Calhoun

E

emphatically declared himself ready to vote both recognition and annexation. That same year, 1836, saw Texas under discussion across the Atlantic in the House of Commons. There 'traditional British policy of supporting Mexico as a barrier against the United States' [58a] had appeared in Canning's measures as early as 1825 and had been steadily continued by British foreign ministers. Meanwhile, British commercial interests in Mexico were greatly extended and Mexican trade grew. England, though recognizing the instability of Mexican politics, hoped, after 2nd March, 1836, and the Texas Declaration of Independence, for Mexico's early reconquest of her truant province. This was natural—peace meant protection of England's own economic interests in Mexico. On 5th June, 1836, one Barlow Hoy had called Commons' attention to the existence of slavery and the slave-trade in Texas and asked if the government intended interference to check these evils. Palmerston replied that Texas was in a state of revolt, thus implying that the moment was inopportune for Britain.[49a] Later, in August 1836, Hoy, speaking for the opposition, introduced a motion instructing the government to take such measures as might be necessary to secure the fulfilment of existing treaties with Mexico 'and prevent the establishment of slavery and traffic in slaves in the province of Texas.' [49b] Hoy's meaning was 'that Mexico's ability to pay British creditors would be lessened if Texas became independent.' [59a] In a speech in support of his motion, Hoy emphasized as threefold the essential interests of Britain in Mexico: the large amount of British money invested in British trade; the danger of the annexation of Texas by the United States, whereby the latter would acquire vast commercial advantages; and the probability that slavery would be permanently established in Texas. Concluding, Hoy urged Palmerston to send a naval force to aid Mexico in recovering control of Texas. Hoy's motion was supported by other speakers such as Henry G. Ward, formerly Britain's first minister to the Republic of Mexico, who urged that action was necessary not only to defend the commercial interests of Great Britain but in order that England should not sit idly by and 'let the United States pursue a policy of aggrandisement and annex Texas, thereby shutting us out of the Gulf and trade with Mexico' and, perhaps, permitting the United States to annex Texas and, thereby, perpetuate slavery in the United States.

Palmerston replied that Hoy's motion was partly both unnecessary and premature and that the government considered action not then necessary. Furthermore, the foreign secretary expressed disbelief in the existence of any extensive African slave-trade with Texas, evaded the question of slavery within Texas and, acknowledging aid to Texas from the people of the

United States as distinguished from the government, declared confidence in the integrity of the United States government. Regarding actual annexation, Palmerston said he did not believe that the United States intended annexation, but, if in the future such intentions became apparent, he declared that both the House and the British public should take notice.

The 1836 debate indicates British attitude toward Texas—public, government, and opposition—for the next several years, namely one of general lack of interest. A bit of British arrogance, that she could if she desired intervene and succeed, is apparent, while the two main points debated in 1836 indicate, even at that early year, the main aspects of later British opposition to American annexation of Texas—namely, the philanthropic element, directed toward the question of slavery in Texas and, second, the commercial, selfish element, turning upon the rivalry of Great Britain and the United States in the commercial development of the Gulf of Mexico. Throughout the years of the annexation struggle, American newspapers frequently cited the points brought forth in the 1836 Commons debate as evidence of the real intentions of Great Britain in Texas, and Palmerston's hint that British interests probably could not permit American annexation irritated a faction of the American public. Examples are cited by Barker, who writes:

> Influential newspapers in New Orleans, Washington, Philadelphia, and New York repeated charges that the Mexican invasions during 1842 were financed by British loans. For example, the Washington *Globe*, quoting the New Orleans *Bee* in April, 1842, declared that British capitalists advanced money to Santa Anna for the invasions, that the British government guaranteed the loans, and that Santa Anna had given the government a mortgage on church property in Mexico for security.
>
> Some papers thought the rumor ridiculous and asked why England should want control of Texas. To this question a writer in the Philadelphia *Public Ledger* replied that British possessions already surrounded the United States, Canada in the North, the Bermudas and Bahamas on the east, islands in the Pacific, and Oregon on the west, and now England wanted a nearer approach to the United States in Texas. Later the *Ledger* said that England had always taken everything she could get and held what she took.[59a]

Apparently, however, England never desired to annex Texas even though she was anxious to prevent its annexation by the United States. In furtherance of her Texas policy, with both its philanthropic and commercial elements and, realizing the increasing importance of the Republic's potentialities to Empire trade, especially as Texas' population increased and as she was recognized by various European powers, England 'did all that it could during 1843-45 to induce Mexico to recognize Texas independence, hoping thereby to lessen the desire of the Texans for annexation.'[59b] The year 1842 marked the development of this definite British foreign-policy with regard to Texas though Aberdeen trod softly, especially during the early months of 1842, whereas his predecessor, Palmerston, had openly favoured an independent Texas, often at the risk of English-Mexican relations.[58b] On 30th August 1841, the Melbourne government, discredited at home by failure in details of home policy and equally discredited abroad by its foreign policy in Egypt and Turkey, fell and, in the new government, Peel became prime minister and Aberdeen replaced Palmerston at the foreign office.

During the remaining and hectic months of Melbourne's government, home affairs, not those of an infant republic across the seas, had occupied Palmerston's attention; and General James Hamilton, who long had interested himself in the affairs of Texas and had acted as a Texan financial agent and recognition negotiator abroad, could secure, at least not until the fall of 1840, but little enthusiasm from Palmerston on the subjects of loans, recognition, and mediation. After several interviews with Palmerston, the Texan agent submitted the outline of a treaty to Palmerston, who placed the Texas question before the cabinet.[58c, 48g] On 13th November, the first of three treaties with England, a treaty of 11 reciprocal, commercial, and navigation articles whose provisions were similar to those ordinarily included in such treaties, was signed. The following day, 14th November, the second treaty, providing for British mediation with Mexico, was signed. By this treaty Great Britain was to offer her mediation in the Texas-Mexico troubles, and, in the event of success within six months after the signing of the convention, Texas was to assume one million pounds sterling of the foreign debts contracted by Mexico before 31st January 1835. Then Agent Hamilton, in order to secure these first two treaties, was forced to accept from Palmerston the third treaty which provided for the suppression of the slave trade and which was in pursuance of England's policy to abolish slavery by signing treaties with the various world nations.[25a] By this treaty certain waters were designated wherein England might search for slaves and take any found to designated ports for condemnation; Texas received the same authority.[47c] Hamilton despatched the first two treaties to Texas, where they arrived early in January 1841. The Senate promptly ratified.[81a, 48h] Hamilton delayed sending the third treaty, for the regulation of the slave trade, a delay which appears both intentional and wise. When Albert T. Burnley, Hamilton's assistant in London, arrived in Texas, Congress had adjourned and the Texas State did not ratify this treaty until January 1842.

Meanwhile, Texas had returned the first two treaties to Palmerston who insisted upon delaying ratification until all three treaties arrived as he suspected that indefinite delay might be the fate of the third treaty.[7bb] By a special protocol, the period for the exchange of ratifications was extended to 1st June 1842, as the Texas Congress was not to meet until October 1841.[48i, 3a] By then a governmental personal change had occurred both in England and Texas. Peel had replaced Melbourne and Aberdeen was Palmerston's successor as foreign secretary. Though English policy towards Texas did not change abruptly, Aberdeen did send William Kennedy to Texas. Kennedy, author of a two-volume work published in London in 1841 on the past and future of the Republic of Texas,[69] was, through this admirably written book, well known both in London and certainly in Texas, where he had spent much of 1839. Though the exact content of his instructions from Aberdeen is unknown, it appears from his letters to Aberdeen that, perhaps, the foreign secretary had sent him as a general agent both to further British interests and to use his influence to secure the passage of the third, slave trade, treaty.[4b] In Texas, too, the government had changed and Houston, successor to Lamar, appointed Ashbel Smith to supersede Hamilton in London.[4c, 42] Smith, arriving in May 1842, immediately attempted to hasten the exchange of ratifications but it was only on 28th July, and after a second protocol had again extended the time limitation, that he was successful.[48j]

Now the treaties were in order and Captain Charles Elliot, who had in August 1841 been notified by Palmerston of his appointment as chargé d'affaires,[4a] had his commission regularized and his appointment confirmed by Aberdeen. On 27th May, 1842, Elliot received an amended commission which gave him the title of consul-general as well as chargé d'affaires.[4d] Aberdeen, in his commission,[4e] instructed Elliot to enjoin 'a careful preservation of the Archives of the Consulate' and, continuing instructions, informed Elliot that

> . . . it will be your duty to avail yourself of every favourable opportunity for collecting and transmitting to me any further useful or interesting Information, relating to Commerce, Navigation and Agriculture, and to any other Branch of Statisticks.
>
> Your Salary has been fixed at £1,200 a year, and will commence ten days before the day of your departure from England; and you are to consider yourself restricted from engaging in Mercantile Pursuits.[4f]

Several days later Aberdeen added a further instruction and told Elliot: 'You will make it your duty to collect and transmit to me Information upon all matters of political Interest and importance in the Republic of Texas.' [4g]

To Anson Jones, Secretary of State of the Republic of Texas, Aberdeen wrote:

> The Queen, My Sovereign, being desirous to cultivate the most friendly Relations between Great Britain and Texas, Her Majesty has appointed Charles Elliot, Esq., a Post Captain in the Royal Navy, to be H.M.'s Consul General in that Country.[4h]

On 1st June, 1842, Elliot, in company with his wife and son, set sail Texaswards in The Royal Steam Packet Company's ship, *Clyde*, for Madeira. From there they took the steamer *Tweed* to New Orleans, arriving 14th August.[4i] Due to heavy seas between New Orleans and Galveston, it was the 23rd before the Elliots reached their new post.[48k] On the 25th, Charles Elliot presented himself to the President and the two men, each an able gossip from rich memories and from richer thoughts for the future, became immediate friends, which they remained throughout Elliot's mission in Texas.[4j]

For some months after his arrival in Texas, Elliot was in ill health [4k] and sent home merely incidental reports largely concerned with his initial, and accurate, opinion that Texas could never be reconquered and that Mexico's predatory border attacks were extremely unwise as they accomplished nothing for Mexico and only irritated Texas. He forwarded to London Houston's handbill, 'Veto Message of the President of the Republic of Texas to the Bill authorizing offensive war against Mexico and for other purposes,' yet, as Houston said, Mexico was 'harrassing and plundering our frontier' and detaining 'in a slavish captivity our fellow citizens of the late Santa Fé Expedition.'[4l] The remainder of these first weeks at Galveston, Elliot sent Aberdeen copies of the *Houston Morning Star* which contained copies of the Treaties between Great Britain and Texas and told of General Woll's activities at San Antonio. Next, he concerned himself with attempts to induce Her Majesty's Treasury to grant him an allowance 'in consideration of the extraordinary expense I had incurred whilst acting as Her Majesty's Plenipotentiary in China';[4m] the Treasury refused and he was reminded of the grant, in addition to his salary, of 'one pound a day allowance to meet additional expenses.'[5a] Also he was occupied with the respectful and jealous requests of the citizens of Matagorda for recognition similar to Galveston's.[4n] To Mr Ward Ingram and other citizens of Matagorda, Elliot adroitly replied regretting that 'it is not in my power to make a British Consular appointment for the Port of Matagorda. But I am sensible of its growing importance and it will afford me pleasure to move Her Majesty's Government to comply with your request.'[4o] Meanwhile, he was constantly reminded of 'the inhuman pillaging in Texas' (by

70

Mexico) about which 'the whole civilized world is concerned.' [5b] Elliot, reporting to the Foreign Office, praised Houston's moderate policy toward Mexico 'in spite of Indian troubles' and 'the activities of Mexican frontier robbing parties.' [5c] The home office, apparently, held to the same opinion for, at almost the same date, Aberdeen informed Elliot of his desire that President Houston be informed of

> . . . the satisfaction which Her Majesty's Government have derived from the moderation of his (Houston's) Language and Proceedings with regard to Mexico.
> You will, at the same time, repeat to him the firm determination of Her Majesty's Government to employ their best exertions to put a stop to the fruitless and desultory War which still exists between Mexico and Texas. . . . [5d]

In view of the extremely alarming border war, Elliot, considering safety, asked permission from London to maintain the Consulate at Galveston, instead of Austin. Aberdeen laid the Elliot-Addington correspondence on this subject before the Foreign Office and informed Elliot that

> . . . under the circumstances therein stated (a letter of Elliot to Addington), H.M.'s Govt. approve of your residing usually at Galveston, instead of Austin; and in the present unsettled state of the Country, I leave it to your discretion to decide, according to circumstances, wherever you may consider your presence most conducive to the Interest intrusted to your charge. [5e]

On 26th March 1842, Houston had issued a 'Blockade Proclamation' extending to

> . . . all the Ports of Mexico from Tobasco in the State of Tobasco to Matamoras in the State of Tamaulipas, and comprising the mouth of the Rio Grande del Norte, and the Brazos Santiago, and all the estuaries, inlets, and passes on the said Eastern Coast of Mexico. . . . [5f]

England, alarmed about the safety of her own ships in the West Indian waters, informed Elliot on 16th July that England 'must observe a strict neutrality in Mexican-Texan affairs.' [5g] Since 1st July, Aberdeen had been in conference with the Admiralty, much concerned over 'Texas' blockade of the Mexican Eastern Coast as far as Vera Cruz' and anxious 'that H.M.'s ships in West Indian waters must be protected and be cautious and that, apparently, the blockade was effective.' [5h] Later, in the records, a copy of Houston's 'Revocation of the Blockade' is included, undoubtedly with a large sigh of relief on the part of the Foreign Office. [5i]

By November of 1842, Elliot's health had much improved and his letters and despatches to England, though because of his illegible penmanship they involve laborious effort to decipher, afford highly rewarding contemporary information upon conditions in Texas. Elliot was an enthusiastic

71

and keen observer, both of men and things, and his intimacy, not only with the citizens of the Republic but with the leading men of the government, Houston, Jones, Ashbel Smith, and others, make his writings a rich mine in which to quarry. Many of Elliot's letters were sent to Addington, his personal friend and a permanent and influential under-secretary in the Foreign Office.[5] These letters, sparkling in the mausoleum of official records and publications, were devoted to the evolution and realization of a grand plan involving Great Britain's assistance in creating Texas as a strong, independent state, thereby assuring permanent British interests in Texas.[5j] Though nominally personal, their incorporation in a volume containing official despatches is indicative that they were regarded as official correspondence, though they were not addressed to the Foreign Secretary.

Meanwhile, Elliot wrote his first lengthy despatch to Aberdeen. This report,[5k] dated at Galveston 2nd November 1842, began:

> If I may presume to offer an opinion upon the general subject of this country, thus brought under your Lordships notice, I should say that its present critical condition arises from departure from that steady abstinence from aggressive War on Mexico, either by land or sea, which has always been General Houston's policy, in or out of place (!); I cannot say power, for this Government is without force or means.[5l]

Continuing his observations, Elliot informed the Foreign Office that, in his own opinion, Texas' creation of a Texas marine, at enormous expense, was unnecessary, for Mexico had no marine to molest Texas and no merchant ships to capture; that the Texan vessels' only purpose was 'to trouble and provoke friendly neutrals, to incite the foreign merchants, connected with the trade of Mexico, and to stimulate the supineness of the Government of that country, by futile manifestations before their ports.' [5l] Consequently, 'the result has been the creation of the present Mexican marine.'

That inflammatory topic, the Santa Fé Expedition, was a venture, reported Elliot, which was 'undertaken without knowledge of the country, without military resources, and without discipline,' and its consequences

> . . . were the surrender of the whole party on the threshold of the Mexican territory, the incitement of the frontier population, ill affected to their own Government, and not ill neighbours to the Texians, retaliatory incursions on the part of the Mexican Government, the strengthening of the confidence of that Government, and its troops in their capacity to contend with this people, the organization of a corps armed with the same description of weapon, (the rifle) and finally, something little short of the breaking up of the whole Western Country of Texas.[5l]

Furthermore, Elliot had concluded, during his first several months in Texas, that

> When the Character of the Mexican Government and people is considered it seems reasonable to think that adherence to wiser courses, would have long since made it a matter of indifference to Texas whether Mexico acknowledge its independence or not, for a profitable and growing forced trade with its North Eastern Provinces of Mexico was inevitable.[5l]

This natural evolution the Mexican Government could not have disturbed successfully, without great local commotion, but could have regulated by a treaty of peace. Elliot offered, in support of his view, the fact 'that traders accompanied the Mexican force that surprised San Antonio,' September past, and that these traders bought up, at handsome prices, all merchandise deposited in San Antonio, and 'carried it back under the protection of the retiring force.' [5l] Elliot reported that nothing certain of San Antonio's fate was known and that 'this lone circumstance' would enable Aberdeen to 'judge of the condition of this country in respect to military vigilance.' [5m] If the Texans in 1842 would practice Houston's strategy of 1836 and draw the enemy far within Texas, 'it is hard to believe that an opposing force, taken at proper advantage, would succeed in getting out of it.' [5n] Concluding his despatch, Elliot observed that 'the heavy rains and tempestuous weather of the last month and September have seriously damaged the crops of this year' [5o] and contributed additional difficulties to the already plentiful troubles of the Republic.

To his friend Addington, Elliot's letters were in a different vein. The first, dated 15th November,[5p] contains Elliot's eulogy of Houston's remarkable career which, though already known in the United States, was introduced into England by Kennedy and, during Elliot's four years in Texas, was to become, through Elliot's letters home, a subject of uncommon interest and comment in England. Houston's story, as unfolded by Elliot, indeed, had great influence in making Texas and Texan conditions known in Great Britain and, consequently, in stimulating British activities in the Republic. Elliot's estimate of Houston was based upon numerous personal conferences, for the two became intimate friends.[56] The Scot considered that only one man was capable of founding Texas as a great and independent state, Sam Houston. The one corroding evil in this promising state, the chief obstacle to its future greatness and independence, believed Elliot, was the institution of slavery. Elliot's plan, as he unfolded it in this 15th November letter to Addington, called for the extinction of slavery, a measure which, combined with its philanthropical aspects, would result in manifold and great practical advantages for British commerce. He explained to Addington:

> My scheme supposes another Convention in this Country.—Slavery to be

73

abolished; the entire abolition of political disabilities upon people of Colour, *perfectly free trade* to be declared to be a fundamental principle; the right of voting to depend upon a knowledge of reading and writing, and a pretty high money contribution to the State, . . . stringent legislation against squatting, in the form of a land tax and otherwise; improvements upon the well established failure and folly of a yearly elected Legislature and other liberality of the rhodo-montade school. It seems to be scarcely doubtful that the Northern and North-Eastern parts of Mexico, from Tampico on the North-East Coast, to San Blas on the West (involving the most important parts of the Country) would soon find it their interest to join a state founded upon such principles, or at all events constrain their own Government into the adoption of an equally liberal scheme of commercial policy. Foreign Merchants, Foreign Capital, and foreign enter-prise and principles would soon find their way into these great and rich regions by peaceful means, and the power of the United States on this Continent would be gradually balanced, and yet without motive for collision; Indeed it seems possible enough that the North Eastern States would not be disturbed to see the power of the South and West effectually limited and a bound marked beyond which Slavery could not advance.[59]

Thus was Elliot advocating and emphasizing the commercial advantages to Great Britain that would result from the erection of a powerful and independent new republic, Texas. Moreover, Elliot's fantastic scheme included the immodest notions that the Texans who, in truth, anticipated annexation to the United States, land of their genesis, would abolish slavery, guarantee free trade, and enfranchise the blacks. Even more irrational was his belief that Mexico would quietly accept a boundary line so extended as to give the Anglos a large slice of Mexico; or that the border Mexicans, whose chief occupation had been guerrilla warfare with their northern neighbours, would voluntarily subject themselves to Texan authority. Yet Elliot sincerely believed that a British loan, compensating the slaveholders in Texas, was the means of his Utopian end. In closing his letter to Addington, however, he reminded the under-secretary that all this constituted his private plan and that, of course, officially and publicly, he would take the ground that Great Britain, though abhorring slavery for herself, had neither desire nor intention to interfere with it in other countries.

This suggestion of Elliot, that Britain operate in Texas to secure the abolition of slavery there, is of significant interest. Besides this initial instance of British official expression of this aim, it is inconceivable to think that Elliot's letters to Addington did not reach the desks of Aberdeen and others in the Foreign Office. Also, the topic of the origin of the grand plan invites attention. In view of the increasingly intimate, and mutually admiring, amity between Elliot and President Houston, surely the two discussed at length the plan for the Republic. If such a plan were Houston's idea, was his object, by a clever and intentional flaunting of the close English-Texas relationship, thereby suggesting England's interference in Texas, to frighten the United States into hastening annexation? Such is the traditional theory [73] but, apparently, Houston did not so manœuvre until 1843 for, until the Elliot-Addington letter of November 1842, no trace of the suggestion by British officials that Texas abolish slavery is found; nor until then had there been suggestion to Mexico that she make the abolition of slavery in Texas a condition of recognition. Therefore Elliot's scheme, expressed as it was soon after his acquaintance with Houston, may well be significant and, moreover, may be conclusive evidence of Houston's desire to make of England a potent tool. Yet it should be remembered, in defence both of Houston's integrity and of his sincere desire for an independent Texas, that, logically, the man might have found in England and in Elliot confederates in his cause. In further support of this latter theory are the letters sent by Ashbel Smith, in London, to Houston. Smith, writing Houston twice on 3rd October 1842, reported English admiration of Houston's veto of the Invasion of Mexico Bill, unhappily informed the President that the Lords Treasury had released the 'Montezuma,' stressed England's desire for Texan-Mexican peace, enumerated England's manifold interests in Texas, reported that ones Hall and Burnley were in London 'selling Texas land,' blasted out at 'spurious land claims,' related the activities of Dr Daniel J. Carroll in England 'to introduce immigrants into the Red River Colony,' and also those of S. Converse, Esq., to introduce immigrants into Texas, and informed Houston that England's great fear was that Texas would 'join the Union.' [42a] On 21st October, Smith wrote Houston of the 'political and commercial intimacy of Great Britain and Mexico,' of Britain's desire for Texan independence and her fear that Mexico intended to invade Texas, of Texas' desire for a British loan, and of the departure from London for Texas of the Count de Craymael to succeed Alphonso de Saligny, the loudly denounced French chargé d'affaires to Texas.[42b] The thread of potential and successful French interference in Texas runs through the Smith-Houston correspondence. On 30th December, Smith wrote from Paris that he was 'with Aberdeen maintaining the rights of Texas' and conversing in this aim with such 'individuals as Saligny, Guizot, Villemain, and Philibeaucourt.' [42c] On 1st February 1843, still in Paris, Smith elaborated upon Texas' relations with France;[42d] some days later, on 11th April, he reported presentation of his opinion of Texas to Leopold of Belgium.[42e] By 1st August of the same year, Smith was elated over his observation that 'Texan-English relations had improved by peace' [42f] (between Texas and Mexico?) and, on 30th October, he was noting (with lament?) both the popularity of the Count de Narbonne's *Monsieur Violet's Adventures in Texas* and the rising interest of King Louis Philippe's interest in Texas.[42g] On 27th November, Smith in Paris reported discussion of commercial treaties with Saligny, speculated upon a treaty with Spain, noted 'Henry Castro's superintendency of a ship-load of colonists from Antwerp,' reported 'visits of the Messiers Hue and Craffin, agents of Martinique and Guadalupe, to New Orleans to counteract abolitionists scheme,' and told Houston of the 'annexation furor in Europe.' [42h] By June 1844, Smith, back in London, reported his recent talks with the Pope about 'religious conditions in Texas' and his negotiations with the Prince de Ligne, Belgian minister to London, for commercial treaties, and, again, emphasized the European annexation furor.[42i] The date 7th April 1845,[42j] is the date of Smith's eloquent requiem on annexation though, as late as 1848,[42k] from Galveston, and 1851,[42l] from London, he lamented the passing of the great Republic. And during all these years, years of Elliot's mission to Texas and years succeeding the final annexation of Texas by the United States, both Charles Elliot and Lord Aberdeen believed in Houston's sincere desire to establish an independent state.

In his 15th November letter to Addington, Elliot enclosed a personal letter from Houston, dated 5th November, in which Elliot was requested to secure permission from Aberdeen to act as the agent of the Republic of Texas in securing peace from Mexico.[5p] Elliot, on 11th December, replied to Houston that he would quite willingly act in that capacity, provided London granted such authority. In the same letter, he reported that the belligerent tone of Ashbel Smith's communications [6,78] on the 'Montezuma' affair had greatly angered Houston, who had asked Elliot to express to Aberdeen the sincere regret and courteous apologies of the Texan Government in regard to the whole matter. In this same 11th December letter, Elliot further elaborated upon his visionary plan and speculated upon the increasing possibility of its realization. A few days later, on 16th December, he was troubled by a wave of annexation rumours surging over Texas and wrote Addington that delay in the execution of his plan would be fatal and that he, Elliot, could not

> . . . help thinking that money lent to put an end to slavery in a South West direction in America and to give a place and position to the coloured races, would render as profitable returns as money spent in fortresses and military works on the Northern frontier of the United States.[5q]

Throughout the Elliot-Addington correspondence, Elliot emphasized those facets of his plan currently popular in Victorian England, *videlicet* the humanitarian and philanthropic. Yet he always stressed the potential and distinct financial advantages to British trade. On 28th December, writing one of his more interesting letters to Addington, he carefully analyzed President Tyler's annual message to Congress and interpreted it as the United States' warning to England to keep her hands off both Texas and Oregon. Furthermore, Elliot expressed his opinion that the recent treaty of Washington, signed by Ashburton and Webster, was far from a permanent settlement of the points in dispute between Great Britain and the United States. This treaty, resumed Elliot, in his apparent attempt to invigorate his scheme for an independent Texas, was considered as a mere respite in the United States and was certain to foretell the renewal of a policy hostile to Great Britain.

The incident of the tripartite intervention, subsequently overestimated both as to its importance in a study of English-Mexican-Texan relations and as to its indication of a selfish line of British policy, remains to be mentioned for the year 1842. England, France, and the United States were to urge peace upon the government of Mexico. Ashbel Smith, at London, had been instructed [48l] by Secretary of State Anson Jones to propose such intervention to both England and France and Smith had secured from Guizot, in Paris, a promise to join in such tripartite intervention.[65c] But Aberdeen, 15th October, declined the measure on the reasoning that, while relations between England and Mexico were friendly, those between the United States and Mexico were critical; therefore, he did not desire sacrifice of Anglo-Mexican relations by joining with the United States and France. Also, Aberdeen reminded Smith and the French ambassador in London that, already in that year 1842, England twice had proposed to Mexico that she recognize Texas, and Mexico twice had refused. Evidently, neither Jones, Smith, nor the French had much hope in such a measure but did consider it worth an effort. Aberdeen's conclusions are apparent in his reply to the proposal: Mexico already had refused to accept the advice of England, the European power most friendly with her; Mexico would not be likely to accept a proposal made by three powers. Hence Aberdeen concluded, if the plan were so unpromising, England was justified in guarding her friendship with Mexico.

Such caution on Aberdeen's part and, apparently, a sense of security as well characterize London's attitude toward Texas, during the last months of 1842. Aberdeen had no fear of American annexation or, at least, he believed that there was no immediate danger from the United States. Elliot, on the other hand, was on the ground and ardently elaborating, in

77

his letters to Addington, upon his grandiose scheme for an independent
Texan State and urging vigorous British action in support of Texan
independence. But the Foreign Office had been unhurried even in its
commission to the intrepid William Kennedy who, during the fall of
1841, had pleaded with Aberdeen that England must be active because

> . . . a new revolution has broken out in Mexico—military associations for the
> purpose of overthrowing British rule and influence in North America have been
> formed, from Mexico to Missouri,—the planters of Cuba are growing impatient
> of British interference in the Slave Trade. . . .[3]

and he, Kennedy, now, after his travels through the United States and
his sojourn in Texas, was convinced that

> . . . unless English influence be employed in raising up a stable independent
> power in the South-Western, and North-Western frontiers of the Union, a very
> few years will suffice to place the whole of the territory they covet under the
> Sovereignity (sic) of the United States.—There lies the danger to the Maritime
> and Commercial supremacy of Great Britain.[3]

These opinions Aberdeen had received and, finally, in November 1841,
had given Kennedy some class of a commission to go to Texas and report
upon general affairs there for the benefit and information of the British
Government. The year 1842 closed with Kennedy not yet arrived in Texas
and Elliot, through his personal letters to Addington, reporting to Aberdeen.
Perhaps British complacency was augmented further, in 1842, by the
publication in London of James Silk Buckingham's volumes, *The Slave
States of America.*[64] Though an ardent abolitionist, Buckingham could
foresee only disappointing outcome for the abolition movement; moreover,
he penned, for British official and public reading, his own opinions that
continuance of British abolition agitation, in addition to being both hopeless and useless, might embitter severely Great Britain's relations with the
United States. None the less, like Kennedy, Buckingham believed in the
future greatness of Texas and in her importance to British interests; but,
unlike Elliot, he wrote that desire for annexation in slaveholding Texas
was waning. But the same months had witnessed a decidedly different
attitude on the part of Sir Richard Pakenham, British minister to Mexico.
His reports to London indicated utter indifference to the Texan independence movement. Meanwhile, Ashbel Smith, at the Texas London
Legation, was, by able diplomacy and personal charm, daily enhancing
his Republic's potentialities upon European states, particularly England.[6]
In this admirable cause, Smith was aided in favourably impressing Aberdeen
by President Houston's letters, sent through his personal friend, Elliot,
directly to the Foreign Secretary. So anxiety over American annexation

was expressed by only one man, Elliot. And he foresaw the probability or possibility and unwaveringly urged his annexation fears as reason for British activity. But Aberdeen continued to feel secure, for the moment.

The year 1842 closed with Aberdeen refusing to join France and the United States in a triple intervention to be urged upon Mexico. The Foreign Secretary had decided that independent action by England, aided possibly by France, was a wiser policy and one from which Mexico would be more likely to make peace. Consequently, both the English and French ministers in Mexico received like instructions. But to Pakenham the procedure appeared useless and, after consulting with the French minister, he reported his disobedience to Aberdeen on the ground of the inutility of the act and, surprisingly, received Aberdeen's approval for withholding the matter from Mexico.[58d] Soon thereafter Pakenham was recalled to London, promoted to the ministry at Washington, and replaced in Mexico City by Percy Doyle, a less capable man who, unfortunately, was to conduct the delicate armistice negotiations of 1843 between Mexico and Texas.

The first quarter of 1843 found Elliot still devoted to his plan for a great and slave-free Texas where British commercial advantages would be enormously extended. His letters to Addington were penned in this vein and, frequently, he stressed the danger of Texan annexation to the United States and entreated England to press Mexican-Texan peace, and thus prevent annexation.[7a] In this effort, Elliot enjoyed President Houston's support for, on 24th January 1843, Houston wrote Elliot urging that England force Mexico to make peace, and that speedily.[7b] Houston's letter which Elliot forwarded to Aberdeen, explained

> There is a subject now mooting in Texas which it seems to me will appeal directly to Her Majesty's Government. I mean that of annexation to the United States. Some of our journals are much in favor of the measure. I find from the uncertitude of our situation that nine-tenths of those who converse with me are in favor of the measure upon the ground that *it will give us peace*. Upon this point of our national existence I feel well satisfied that England has the power to rule.[7b]

In this 'personal' letter to his friend, Elliot, President Houston further averred that the whole United States was rapidly becoming a unit, with both political parties favouring annexation and that, should annexation occur, the territory annexed would include not only Texas but the Bay of San Francisco and the Pacific Coast in general! And,

> ... Annexation is to be a question with the political parties and aspirants in the United States. My own opinion is that both parties will advocate the policy. To defeat this policy it is only necessary for Lord Aberdeen to say to Santa Anna,

'Sir, Mexico must recognize the independence of Texas.' Santa Anna would be glad of such a pretext. He could then say to the Mexicans–You see how I am situated. I cannot go to war with England, our last friend, with a probability of war with the United States and France.[7b]

Generally, this February 1843 letter of Houston to Elliot is considered as the frank expression of Houston that marked a definite change of policy on his part. Soon after becoming president for the second time, Houston had reopened annexation by instructing the Texas chargé d'affaires in Washington to find occasion to inform the government that Texas would consider the subject.[59c] On 23rd December 1842, Isaac Van Zandt informed Houston that both President Tyler and the majority of his cabinet were anxious for annexation but dubious that an annexation treaty could secure a two-thirds majority for ratification in the Senate. The inference, subsequently, was that, by February 1843, Houston dropped annexation and, thereafter, sought to arouse the antagonism of the United States to Great Britain in order to force the United States to make overtures to Texas.[73a] Yet the Elliot-Houston correspondence, both before February 1843 and following, fails to indicate change in Houston's policy. Houston had always, from the day of Elliot's arrival in Texas, accented Texan independence and voiced his desire for British intervention to secure peace. And Houston's assertions to Elliot of his desire for an independent Texas were as energetic before as after his overtures to Tyler were made and rejected. The correspondence between the two Washingtons was largely desultory in nature until July 1843 when Houston instructed Secretary Jones to write Van Zandt that his 1842 instructions were withdrawn because Houston hoped to make peace with Mexico, after which the United States Senate might prefer ratification of a treaty to annexation, involving danger of war with Mexico.[59d] But Van Zandt was simply to say that his earlier instructions were suspended; and Tyler inferred what Houston intended—namely, recognition of independence by Mexico, guaranteed by England, would make Texas less eager for annexation.

Elliot, meanwhile, receiving from London no reply to his letters which glowingly advocated ardent British activity in Texan affairs, became disquieted and decided to shift emphasis from the abolition of slavery in Texas to the necessity of immediate English pressure upon Mexico for recognition, in order to preserve the commercial interests of Great Britain and prevent American annexation. In this channel, Elliot composed long and engaging accounts of the crude, but ever good and practical, Texans whom he depicted as

... rough, and wild, but their consistancy and courage are admirable. I hardly know any more fearful and indeed humiliating subject of reflection than the comparative helplessness of our own poor English people, when we find them thrown amongst these scheming, enterprising, and it is most distressing to add, almost invariably much better informed persons than themselves. The truth is that the poorer classes of English people are broken in, or should I say broken *down* to do but one thing in the world . . . in this country they make but sorry work of it in taming the wilds, compared with the American races. The training of our political and social mechanism (and my experience has taught me, military too) unfits men for rough uses and reverses. It must all work together perfectly *smoothly* and *successfully*, or it will hardly work at all. These strange people *jolt* and *jar* terrifically in their progress, but *on* they do get, and prosper too, under circumstances when our people would starve and die.[7c]

On 29th March, Elliot learned of the Robinson plan, intended to secure a Texan-Mexican armistice as a forerunner of ultimate peace. J. W. Robinson, captured in San Antonio in March 1842, had been sent to Mexico City, where he obtained an audience with Santa Anna, to whom he reported that a large party in Texas desired annexation to Mexico on terms of local self-government and nominal Mexican sovereignty. Santa Anna had commissioned Robinson to make overtures to the Texan government, releasing the prisoner for that mission. Soon afterwards, Santa Anna fell ill and nothing came of the plan from Mexico but Robinson, upon reaching Texas, informed Houston of Santa Anna's desire for an armistice. Some said the plan was Robinson's ruse to secure liberty, some said Doyle was responsible, and some indicted Elliot. But Elliot's despatches home absolve him for, distinctly distrusting Santa Anna, he wrote Aberdeen only incidentally of the Robinson plan and prolonged his despatch to report both rumours and comments of American annexation. On 18th May, Aberdeen, slighting the Robinson armistice plan and devoting his attention to annexation, wrote Elliot:

> With regard to the project for the annexation of Texas to the United States, which has formed the subject of some of your recent communications to this Office, Her Majesty's Government do not think it necessary to give you any Instructions at the present moment on that subject, further than to desire that you will assure the President of the continued interest which the British Government takes in the prosperity and independence of State of Texas: and of their full determination to persevere in employing their endeavours, whenever they see a reasonable hope of success, to bring about an adjustment of the differences still existing between Mexico and Texas, of which they so much lament the continuance.[7d]

Later, in May 1843, Pakenham reached London and presented the projected armistic information to Aberdeen. Pakenham believed that Texas was weary of independence and would, within a few months time, annex herself either to the United States or Mexico. Upon hearing this view from the minister but newly returned from Mexico, Aberdeen despatched instructions both to Elliot in Texas and Doyle in Mexico. He informed Elliot [7e] that he was convinced of Santa Anna's genuineness, and that, apparently, the armistice offer meant virtual independence for the Texans who, surely, would not withhold acceptance over a mere matter of technical sovereignty. But Aberdeen carefully instructed Elliot that Great Britain, though anxious to use her good offices 'in an entirely neutral and impartial sense, in order to bring about a peaceful and equitable adjustment of the differences existing between Texas and Mexico,' would not make herself in any way a party to this transaction or incur any responsibility in regard to it. Yet, while instructing Elliot to urge Texas acceptance of the Robinson plan, Aberdeen instructed Doyle,[58e] acting chargé d'affaires in Mexico, that the plan did not go far enough, that Mexico's best policy would be to make a complete and full acknowledgement of Texas independence, and, interestingly, in this instruction to Doyle of 1st July 1843, Aberdeen, for the first time, launched the abolition question. He wrote Doyle that 'it may deserve consideration whether the abolition of Slavery in Texas would not be a greater triumph, and more honourable to Mexico, than the retention of any sovereignty merely nominal.'[58e]

Meanwhile, Elliot and Houston had been talking together about the Robinson plan and Houston was vehemently opposed to Santa Anna's armistice proposal and to English support of the measure. Elliot, writing Pakenham on 14th April, thinking Pakenham still to be in Mexico, had reported his conversations with Houston.[7f] On 13th May, Houston had written Elliot, repeating his earlier convictions and urging his belief that peace and Texan independence would result only through immediate recognition; and England, by imposing this course upon Mexico, could eliminate the American annexation question. Continuing, Houston 'confided' to Elliot the ever increasing difficulties which annexation caused him, especially as both Texans and Americans appeared increasingly desirous for annexation. On 8th June, when he forwarded this letter to the Foreign Office, Elliot expressed to Aberdeen his desire that it be kept with absolute secrecy.[7g] Replying to Houston, Elliot wrote that he had at no time, either by word or despatch, received instructions from Her Majesty's Government to urge abolition upon the Texan government. Early in June, Elliot, receiving Aberdeen's instructions relating to the Robinson plan, obeyed by presenting a formal document which advised the Texan government to concede Mexican sovereignty, and thus secure the benefits of practical independence.[7h] But at the same time, Elliot, writing Doyle personally, expressed his conviction that only in immediate recognition by Mexico of Texan independence did solution reside. On 24th July, Elliot wrote Jones not advising the concession of Mexican sovereignty but arguing its advantages to Texas.[7i] Elliot's variance to Doyle and to the Texan government is indicative that Elliot, correctly, regarded Aberdeen's instructions as purely perfunctory—Aberdeen had urged upon the states of Texas and Mexico the greatest concessions in the hope that compromise and real conciliation might result. Doyle, on his part, was informed by Santa Ann aof the plan, as Pakenham had previously been; but he lacked instructions from Aberdeen, and although as ambitious as Pakenham for a Mexican-Texan peace, was, for the time, merely reporting the negotiation proceedings in an intermediary fashion. On 13th June, Houston had proclaimed a cessation of hostilities and appointed commissioners to meet those from Mexico. Everyone knew that Mexico would consider no arrangement with Texas which did not recognize Mexican sovereignty; equally well known was the fact that Texas would reject any plan which implied acknowledgment of Mexican sovereignty. Therefore, was Elliot merely Houston's tool to arouse anti-British sentiment in America? Likely no; for it should be remembered that Elliot's statement to Jones was but a formal act in obedience to Aberdeen's instruction concerning the Robinson plan; again, it should be remembered that, personally, Elliot was convinced that between the lines of Aberdeen's formal instructions was written the Foreign Secretary's real intention, namely, to force upon Mexico recognition of Texas; and, finally, the intimate Houston-Elliot friendship indicates that Houston, like Elliot, read the same British intention into Aberdeen's words.

Houston's armistice proclamation was delivered to Santa Anna who, 12th July, ordered General Woll of the Mexican army to cease hostility preparations. Simultaneously, Santa Anna insisted that only through Texan acknowledgment of Mexican sovereignty could final peace be obtained. Doyle regarded Santa Anna's insistence as the necessary result of the Mexican political situation and not as reason for anxiety.[58f] But, in the United States, the Robinson plan and Houston's and Santa Anna's actions were regarded not without anxiety. In June, Texan Secretary of State Jones had alarmed William S. Murphy, the United States agent in Texas, and Murphy reported to the American Secretary of State, Abel P. Upshur, a complete account of the entire matter. Murphy added his personal opinion that President Houston was completely under British influence and no longer thinking of annexation and that he, Murphy, though unable to learn exactly what was afoot in Texas, felt that truly important negotiations were in progress. Upshur reported Murphy's despatch to President Tyler and United States official circles were aroused.

Thus, by summer of 1843, peace appeared probable. But, in order to comprehend the attitude and instructions of the English government, it is necessary to consider foregoing affairs, especially as regards slavery and abolition. Aberdeen, in April, concerned with these matters, sent to Elliot exemplary drafts of treaties for the abolition of the slave trade concluded between Great Britain and Chile.[27a] On 30th May, Aberdeen wrote Elliot desiring Texan population figures for both 1832 and 1842 and answers to specific queries on slavery: the exact number of whites, coloured, male and female; exact yearly number of slaves imported into Texas from Africa or elsewhere; 'is the slave equally protected by law in criminal cases?'; Elliot's opinions regarding the 'treatment of slaves' and 'protection of slaves against masters'; does the slave 'enjoy the same good health and longevity of free persons?'; is 'slave population on the increase or decrease and why?'; is manumission of slaves of common occurrence?; have slave laws become, within the last ten years, more or less favourable to them?; 'is there in Texas a party favourable to the abolition of slavery?'; 'is there any difference in the eye of the law between a free white man and a free coloured man?'; are 'free coloured men ever admitted to offices of the state?' Elliot was instructed to state, in his replies to these queries, whether his answers were drawn from public documents or private information.[27b]

Elliot's slavery report to the Foreign Office, dated at Galveston on 25th July following, shows an objective respect for facts and estimated a 'gross between 60 and 70,000 souls, free between 40 and 50,000 souls; slaves between 15 and 20,000 souls' of which figure there was probably 'a considerable excess of males, both white and coloured'; in 1837, there were 'between 40 and 50,000 souls' gross and 'about 200 African slaves are supposed to have been introduced from Havana in the course of the last ten years.' Elliot continued that, in his opinion, 'there is no reason to believe that there has been any introduction of Slaves for some years past from any other quarter than the United States.' Regarding conditions of the slaves, 'the whole population of Texas is roughly fed, but I have seen no reason to think that the Slave in Texas is ill fed, comparatively considered,' and 'the average Slave is in probably as good health as the free person.' The slave population 'is chiefly employed in the cultivation of cotton, the care of cattle, and in domestic purposes,' which are 'the least injurious modes of employing slaves.' Elliot reminded Aberdeen that 'it must be added that the whole population is exposed to much hardship, and are not generally careful of health.' Increase was 'chiefly by immigration

84

from the United States,' but, especially for the last several years, the 'immigration has been considerably checked, owing to the unsettled state of affairs in Texas.' Manumission was 'very uncommon.' Regarding abolitionists, Elliot reported that 'there is such a party and it's on the increase.' Legally, 'a free coloured man cannot reside in Texas under the Law of the Land, the slave is not protected equally with a free man in criminal cases, there is no protection by law to a slave against his master's ill-conduct,' and 'the evidence of a slave is not received in a Court of Law.' As to the source of his information, Elliot informed the Foreign Office that 'there are no public documents upon such matters, and there never has been a census of the population in Texas.' [27c] Upon receipt of Elliot's despatch, Canning, in the absence of Aberdeen, instructed Elliot that the Admiralty had asked him 'to request the Texian Government to issue warrants enabling ships employed on the coast of Africa to act under the British-Texan Treaty for the Suppression of the Slave Trade.' [27d] In November 1843, Aberdeen ordered Elliot to extend Canning's instructions 'for ships on the North American and West Indian Stations.' [27e]

In July 1843, shortly after a general antislavery convention in London, the World's Convention of Abolitionists, a committee of Texans and Americans convened to discuss the abolition of slavery in Texas and Aberdeen, by then impressed both by Elliot's letters and Pakenham's arrival and communications concerning the Robinson armistice plan, became keenly alive both to the plan and to abolition sentiment. One S. P. Andrews, an ardent abolitionist and temporary resident of Texas, proposed that Britain advance a loan to Texas to purchase and emancipate Texan slaves. On 31st July, Aberdeen's instructions to Doyle referred to the Texan-American abolition committee, the 'Tappan' committee, and transmitted to Doyle the reply of the Foreign Office to the proposals of that committee, namely, if Texas should adopt emancipation, Her Majesty's Government would press that consideration upon Mexico as additional reason for Mexico's acknowledgment of Texas' independence.[58g] Aberdeen, reminding Doyle that the armistice probably foretold the nearness of peace, speculated upon Mexico's wisdom of waiving 'the vain and objectionable condition of nominal supremacy over Texas,' as contained in the Robinson propositions, and substituting that of 'the absolute abolition of the principle of slavery, and properly regulated emancipation of slaves in Texas.' [58g] It is interesting to note that, two months before, in May of 1843, the *New Orleans Bee* had published rumours of Elliot's grand scheme for a re-organized Texas and for the abolition of slavery.[72a] At that time, both Consul Elliot and President Houston were viciously attacked for their

85

'abolition plots,' and the 'plot' did follow the plan advocated in Elliot's letters to Addington. Also, General Duff Green, an American army officer and a Southerner, was in England at the time of the London Abolition Meeting and the Tappan Committee and, evidently, informed Secretary Upshur that England's abolition plans could be used to arouse the friends of American annexation. During the same weeks, Ashbel Smith was writing to the Texan Secretary of State his own opinions of the storm of rumours and was stating to Aberdeen that Texas would never consider abolition.[9a] On 18th August, Parliament debated the theme of the attitude of the British government in this matter of abolition in Texas and Lord Brougham interpellated the ministry on the subject of British interests in Texas.[49c] On the other side of the Atlantic, upon receipt of the various rumours involving British interference in Texas, the United States instructed Edward Everett, the American minister to London, to obtain from Aberdeen a statement relative to his conference with the antislavery committee and, if possible, an announcement of British plans. Later, Everett reported to Washington that Britain had no intention of stirring the Texan slavery question. Perchance, in this tempest of rumours, Elliot, Aberdeen, and Britain herself were suffering the suspicion consequent to Britain's previous colonial activities, as regards slavery and abolition, especially in Latin America, as well as her opposition to the expansion of the United States. Anywise, to Ashbel Smith, on 11th September 1843, Aberdeen stated that the British government had no wish to interfere with Texas, but did continue anxious to see slavery abolished, not only in Texas, but in all parts of the world.[9b]

Yet, Aberdeen had instructed Doyle that Mexican recognition be contingent upon abolition in Texas.[58g] Thus, American suspicions of British policy were not unfounded. By the spring of 1844, annexationists urged that Texas must be annexed not only as a measure of self-protection to the United States against the commercial encroachments of Great Britain but in order to protect the slave interests of the Southern States, so jeopardized by Great Britain's abolitionist advocacy in Texas. And these two points were the ones upon which both Kennedy and Elliot had centred their attention in outlining a plan of British action.[77]

On 14th August, Doyle informed Santa Anna of Houston's acceptance of the armistice and appointment of peace commissioners. This action by Doyle antedated the antislavery Tappan Committee and Aberdeen's subsequent instructions to Doyle that the Robinson Armistice did not go far enough and that Mexico's best policy would be an immediate and complete acknowledgment of Texan independence. At the same time that this subsequent instruction was sent to Doyle, 31st July, a copy was sent to Elliot, together with an account of the Aberdeen-Tappan Committee meeting. Elliot now rejoiced that, perhaps, at long last, his dream was to be realized. He felt that Aberdeen finally was convinced of the necessity for promptly forcing Mexico to make peace. Enthusiastically, he wrote Aberdeen that the proposal for Mexico to acknowledge Texan independence upon the condition of abolition would at once both prevent new slaves being introduced into Texas and would quickly result in the extinction of slavery. Then, he enlarged upon the great advantages to England and told Aberdeen that

> . . . if the principle of free labor can be established here, what with the opportunity of procuring labor from Mexico, and by immigration from other quarters, and the increasing supply and improvement of the staple from India, there would very soon be an end of the remunerative production of Cotton by Slave Labor in the United States.[7j]

Continuing, Elliot informed Aberdeen that with free labour would come free trade and, sensing the death of the American protective system, Elliot predicted the far-reaching effect of the tentative Mexican ultimatum for peace. On 10th October, Elliot wrote Doyle that he trusted that

> . . . Mexico will be true to the great cause of humanity and to Herself, in this momentous occasion. The mere announcement of their just and honorable determination that a land which was free under their rule should not be turned into a Pen of Slaves for the convenience of persons possessing such property in the exhausted Slave States of the North American Union would of itself be a very important step towards the establishment and security of the due and needful weight of Mexico in the affairs of this Continent. They have but to signify that the *sine qua non* conditions of the acknowledgment of Texas by Mexico are decided and approved measures for the early and final disappearance of slavery here, and formal adherence to the declaration of Mexico that the Independence is recognized and understood to be *complete*, whilst Texas remain a Separate Nation, but of no effect in the case that it should annex itself to any other Country, without the consent of Mexico.[7k]

Yet, while enthusiasm and personal convictions caused Elliot to pen such lines, both to England and to Mexico, officially such expressions had no significance. Evidently, Elliot had no private authority or advisor that inspired him, either as the political theorist, dreamer, or philanthropist that he was. Sudden potentiality of wishful dreams merely superseded the diplomat's poise and responsibility, and the mind which impelled the pen was incited by zeal.

Meanwhile, as British influence in Mexico and Texas was being exerted toward peace, via abolition if possible, the United States was attempting to learn the true state of affairs. Secretary Upshur informed William S. Murphy of the Duff Green letter and asked Murphy for information. Murphy, unalarmed about rumours of British abolition plans for Texas, advised the United States not to use the abolition cry against Britain but to attack British policy as attempting to secure from Texas a consent to reannexation to Mexico, a step which, Murphy claimed, could be assailed as a step backward in civil government, religion, and political liberty.[50] But Upshur preferred to charge British interference on the institution of slavery. From England, too, Everett wrote Upshur that England's deep desire was not interference with slavery in Texas, or anywhere else (though she was willing to divert the influential abolitionists, with such speculations), but, rather, England's true Texas policy was to build up a power independent of the United States, a power which could raise cotton enough to supply the world, and that slavery would be a necessary element of such an economy. Everett added that such policy sprang not from enmity to the United States but from love of England, and that so it was with France, too.[73b]

The American offer of an annexation treaty followed. In September 1843, Van Zandt, in Washington, wrote the Texan government that Secretary of State Upshur frequently had discussed annexation and that, apparently, President Tyler contemplated early action. Van Zandt was correct. On 16th October, Upshur proposed opening negotiations for a treaty of annexation and Van Zandt modestly replied that, as he had no instructions on the matter, he would pass it on to the government of the Republic. On 31st October, Elliot, both surprised and chagrined, informed Lord Aberdeen of President Houston's despatch, from the Texan agent to the United States, which gave the outlines of the American offer.[7l] Houston expressed himself as greatly disturbed and told Elliot to inform London that, if Mexico would speedily recognize Texan independence, Texas would decline the American annexation offer. Continuing, Elliot assured Aberdeen that

> . . . Her Majesty's Govt. might rest assured that with the Independence of Texas recognized by Mexico, He (Houston) would never consent to any treaty on this project of annexation to the United States, and He had a conviction that the people would sustain him in that determination. He had formerly been favourable to such a combination; But the United States had rejected the proposals of this Country in its time of difficulty; neither was the subsequent conduct of that Government calculated to induce the Government and people of Texas in this mended state of things, to sacrifice their true and lasting advantage to the policy of party in that Country.[7l]

In these words, then, did Elliot quote Houston and exhibit his own

88

confidence in Houston's sincerity; yet, to Houston, now in such an advantageous bargaining position, Elliot elegantly and concisely replied that he had no instructions as to British policy toward any projected American annexation. In truth, Elliot, invariably an advocate of British action to forestall annexation, and perpetually wary that Texans might favour American annexation, was greatly perturbed. Only the hesitant attitude of the Texans themselves and his own conviction of Houston's sincerity comforted the British consul. With tense concern did he study Houston's instructions to Van Zandt to say to Upshur that the opening of annexation negotiations would cause Mexico to break off the armistice and probably invade Texas, while England would be offended and withdraw her good offices. Houston wanted assurance that a treaty of annexation would be ratified by the Senate and that, meanwhile, President Tyler would undertake to protect Texas from Mexican invasion![59d]

Meanwhile, in Mexico, the unfortunate flag incident had occurred on 28th September 1843, and, for the last months of that year, and until Percy Doyle was replaced by Charles Bankhead as British chargé in Mexico, England's power and influence was at a dangerously low ebb at this critical juncture in Elliot's mission. All efforts to quickly draw the veils of officialdom over the event failed. At a public ball, Doyle, becoming involved in an altercation with Mexican officials, had demanded that an English boat flag, exhibited amongst Texan trophies taken in war, be removed from the wall. The Mexicans refused and all the English withdrew from the ball. The incident created talk even of war between Mexico and England. Doyle broke off diplomatic relations with the Mexican government which, in turn, made an official explanation to Great Britain. Aberdeen accepted the explanation, ordered Doyle to resume diplomatic relations and, hurriedly, despatched Bankhead to replace Doyle in Mexico City. Unfortunately, the Doyle-flag incident already had weakened British influence in Mexico.[XVII, 58h] But, by far most Britons, certainly the colonials, expressed righteous indignation. The *Bermuda Royal Gazette* editor wrote:

> . . . And Mr. Doyle acted rightly when he vindicated that honour, even in the matter of an old tattered ensign, and against a State so unimportant as that of Mexico; for he felt doubtless, that to honour a people in little impertinencies is the surest way of provoking great insults; so that contumely follows contumely, and one fraud another, until a great nation may be effectually derided in its symbols, thwarted in its policy, and cheated out of its just debts, by the upstart impudence of a parvenu Republic.[1a]

XVII The story of the flag incident is in F.O.R. Mexico, 164 and 165; the irritation of British merchants in Mexico, and the inevitable weakening of British Influence in Mexico, is in F.O.R. Mexico, 170.

Additionally unfortunate for the British, at this critical juncture in diplomatic affairs, was the fact that, late in 1843, Elliot fell ill and had to journey to New Orleans to consult a physician. Personally, while under medical care there, Elliot met Henry Clay and the two became friends. Clay assured the Britisher that the United States Senate would block any scheme for Texan annexation. Elliot was relieved and wrote Aberdeen the good news.[7m] The year 1843 closed with Elliot still in New Orleans, but again hopeful for the British cause in Texas; with British Mexican relations almost at war pitch over the flag incident; and with Texas awaiting action on the part of the United States.

The year 1844 brought England's greatest effort to prevent Texan annexation to the United States. In the early months, Elliot informed Aberdeen that he believed that immediate danger of annexation had passed [10a] and that, once again, he felt that Texan peace and independence were imminent.[10b] Moreover, Elliot informed Aberdeen that President Houston, as always, desired independence for the Republic and enclosed a newspaper clipping, quoting a letter dated at Washington in January 1844, from Hugh McLeod who wrote that Duff Green, in Mexico, had

> ... obtained a copy of the mortgage, given by the Govt. of Mexico to the English bond holders, for one hundred and seventy five millions of acres of land in Texas, Chihuhua (sic), New Mexico, Sonora, and the California (sic); twenty five millions of which, are to be located near the Atlantic. From all that he could learn, he was of opinion that Santa Anna sustained by British influence in Mexico would prevail. He was apprehensive, that Mr. Benton's influence in the U.S. Senate would defeat any measure for annexation during the present session of Congress, and believed that it was advisable for Texas to put the western frontier in a position, that would enable us, if necessary, to transfer the war beyond the Rio Grande.[14a]

His next correspondence from Aberdeen granted Elliot leave to journey to New Orleans and remain there 'as long as the health of his infant child required his presence there.' [21a] The Elliots hopefully left for Louisiana where they remained until April when Elliot, alone, made a brief return trip to Texas. Satisfied that the Republic's affairs were the same, he returned to New Orleans where his family and Aberdeen's latest despatches awaited him. On 7th and 15th March, Elliot had informed Aberdeen that his own health was 'seriously dilapidated' and requested permission to absent himself from his post in Texas until his 'health shall have been re-established.' On 18th April, Aberdeen replied and accordingly authorized Elliot 'either to return to England, or to proceed to the United States, or elsewhere for the recovery of your health—taking care, of course to provide for the safe custody of the Official Archives during your absence.' [21b] Upon receipt of this permission, the Elliots journeyed to Virginia and there, near Washington, Elliot kept in close touch with Sir Richard Pakenham, the new British minister to Washington, and with events at the United States capital. It was the close of 1844 before the Elliots returned to Texas.

Meanwhile, treaty negotiations proceeded. Van Zandt delivered President Houston's questions to the American Secretary of State, Upshur, who replied that the Senate would certainly ratify an annexation treaty; yet Upshur wisely left unanswered Houston's demand for protection of Texas while the treaty was pending. In Texas, Duff Green, as 'consul of the United States for Galveston,' fervidly assured Anson Jones that his government would protect Texas; only later did he have to admit that he had spoken without authority.[14b] But the United States Senate, in spite of Upshur's opinion that he had enough votes pledged to ratify, rejected the treaty. President Houston, having but small apprehension of an invasion by Mexico, temporarily dropped his demand for a pledge of protection and sent J. Pinckney Henderson to Washington to assist Van Zandt. The two Texans had agreed upon a treaty, when Upshur was killed in an accident. John C. Calhoun, believing that he could assure and hasten annexation, was induced by President Tyler to take Upshur's post. The Texans now renewed their demand for protection and Tyler and Calhoun, aware that only Congress could declare war, did go as far as the constitution permits when the President, 11th April 1844, ordered a naval force to the Gulf and the army to the southwestern frontier. The following day, the treaty was signed.

The treaty declared as its purpose annexation to further the mutual security and prosperity of the United States and Texas. Texas ceded her public land and public property, such as naval and military equipment, and her right to levy tariff duties; the United States agreed, after territorial status had been fulfilled, to annex Texas as a state. The United States assumed the obligation to pay the public debt of the Republic, up to ten million dollars, and the boundary of Texas as laid down by the Congress of the Republic in 1836—the Rio Grande from mouth to source and then northward to the 42nd parallel of latitude—was the boundary claimed by Texas in 1844; yet, by the treaty, the United States might make boundary adjustments with Mexico.

President Tyler, 22nd April 1844, sent the annexation treaty, whose terms were flagrantly unfavourable to Texas, to the Senate.[7o] In his message of transmittal, he emphasized the benefits to be derived by all sections of the United States from rightful annexation and indicated the danger of British interference, if annexation failed. Texas' immense agricultural, commercial, and manufacturing value to West, East, and South would benefit the United States' destiny. In addition, the South would benefit by security from interference with slavery either by domestic or foreign agents. Should annexation fail, Texas would seek friendship elsewhere. Mexico, continued Tyler, had no right to consider annexation an act of aggression, for Texas had maintained her independence for eight years.

The treaty could not have been presented at a more ill-omened time than April 1844. The previous fall, in October 1843, President Tyler had assured President Houston that the Senate would ratify promptly, and former President Jackson had written Houston from the Hermitage that he was assured of 39 senatorial ayes, while only 35 were required. But, six months later, by April 1844, when the treaty went to the Senate, the national conventions were on the eve of nominating presidential candidates and annexation was a controversial subject. Until 8th June, the Senators hesitated and then defeated the treaty 35 to 16, 15 of the negation votes coming from Whig senators of the slave states. The Whigs were solidly against it, as were the northern states, all but five uniting to defeat the measure.[74a] Henry Clay, the outstanding Whig and their candidate, had compromised on the annexation issue, declaring against it in hopes of satisfying the Northern opponents of annexation; at the same time, in an effort to gain Southern support, he declared that under different conditions, that is, without the hazard of a foreign war and with general concurrence of the Union, annexation might be accomplished. Van Buren, the chief candidate for the Democratic candidacy, unfortunately spoke against annexation in a preconvention statement, and so antagonized the Southern Democrats that they prevented his nomination and Polk, a Southern annexationist, received the nod. Even Senator T. H. Benton, the Missourian advocate of annexation for a quarter of a century, voted to reject the treaty. Congress adjourned shortly thereafter and the annexation topic thus became live campaign and election fodder. On 10th June, President Tyler, desirous of leaving annexation before the nation, sent all the Texas papers to the House and asked for annexation by an act of Congress.

Meanwhile, the London Foreign Office had avidly watched the Washington picture. The satisfaction resulting from the cessation of Mexican-Texan hostilities had been but short-lived, owing to the American annexation proffer which so promptly followed.[21c] Aberdeen, for a time, had been content that the Texan refusal to act until the United States Senate formally sanctioned annexation was a good omen; but, as the months of 1844 rolled by, he realized that, in America and in the new

Republic certainly, diplomatic affairs could and did change momentarily. In the summer of 1843, his conference with the anti-slavery committee had resulted in much irritation in the United States and he attempted to quell the clamour he had aroused. On 2 6th December 1843, he instructed Pakenham to inform Upshur correctly of the Foreign Office's attitude and these letters, afterwards known as the Calhoun-Pakenham correspondence,[55] throw light on the British attitude. The key letter,[21d] that of Aberdeen to Pakenham on 9th January 1844, was written after Aberdeen received President Tyler's annual message to Congress outlining an annexation policy, and hinting at British interference in Texas. Aberdeen indignantly expressed his wrath at the tone of the Tyler message and instructed Pakenham so to inform Upshur. Concluding, Aberdeen wrote:

> I have now to desire that in executing that Instruction, you will take the opportunity of observing to the Secretary of State, that the language of the President, when speaking of the measures which the U. States may hereafter have occasion to adopt, ill accords with this condemnation of the supposed designs of other powers. You will state to Mr. Upshur, that H.M.'s Govt. would have been glad if they could have discovered in the Message greater evidence of that disinterested policy, the presumed absence of which in other quarters, the President had thought necessary to call to the Notice of his Countrymen.[21d]

This instruction was never presented by Pakenham, who regarded his task of enlightening Upshur as extremely unsavoury, and, therefore, this particular letter was not published. It elucidates Aberdeen's surprise and displeasure at the unjust and unwarranted insinuations in Tyler's message. As usual, the Foreign Secretary stressed Great Britain's denial of any attempt to secure abolition in Texas by improper or indirect methods, elaborating upon Britain's imbedded anti-slavery theories. Thus, cleverly, was it possible to distract attention in the United States from any definite British effort to prevent United States annexation of Texas. Abolition was the theme of the correspondence, but British anti-annexation plans were the considerations. Tyler's message, perhaps, motivated Aberdeen's next move, namely a joint British-French effort to prevent annexation. On 12th January 1844, Aberdeen instructed Cowley in Paris [21e] to inform the French Government of Tyler's message and to remind France that, because both France and England had recognized the independence of Texas and had entered into treaties with the Republic, Her Majesty's Government presumed 'that the Government of France would not any more than that of Great Britain, look with indifference upon any measure, by which Texas should cease to exist as a separate and independent State' and that, at the same time, 'it is sufficiently evident that the future annexation of Texas to the United States is contemplated by the President.'[21e] Aberdeen, concluding, desired ascertainment from M. Guizot 'whether the views of H.M.'s Govt. on this subject are shared by the Government of France' and, if so, Cowley was to

> . . . propose that the Representatives of the two Govts. at Washington and in Texas, should be instructed to hold the same language, deprecating all inter-ference on the part of the United States in the affairs of Texas, or the adoption of any measure leading to the destruction of the separate existence of that State (Texas): at the same time, warning the Texian Govt. not to furnish the United States with any just cause of complaint, and encouraging them to look to the preservation of their independence, as the best security for their ultimate prosperity, both political and commercial.[21e]

Apparently, England was prepared, if France acquiesced, to prohibit annexation directly. Aberdeen believed that the combined efforts of two formidable European states would prevent annexation, without resort to force, and, moreover, Aberdeen underestimated both the American annexationist fever and the boldness of the venturesome United States government. Cowley's reply to Aberdeen, on 15th January, reveals that France was in perfect agreement with England.[21f] The plan, of course, presupposed immediate Mexican recognition of Texan independence, thus depriving Texas of reason for accepting annexation.[41, 71]

Representatives to the Republic from England and France, Charles Elliot and Alphonso de Saligny, and Pakenham in Washington, received notice of Aberdeen's plan and Ashbel Smith in London was asked if Texas would agree to France and England forcing Mexico to recognize Texas. Smith said, personally, he believed that such a plan would carry if permanent peace were insured and if Texas were given the advantages of a commercial treaty with Spain permitting trade with Cuba.[48m, 75a]

After rejection by the Senate, Texas redoubled its demand for fulfilment of the protection pledge and Houston told Elliot that he was done with annexation. Consequently, annexationists in the United States became more anxious. In September 1844, Houston instructed Anson Jones, then secretary of state and president-elect of Texas, to order Ashbel Smith, minister from Texas to London and Paris, to conclude certain commercial arrangements with England and France. Houston was certain that these instructions would reach other than top-drawer channels but Jones took them seriously, did not forward them to Smith and, on the back of Houston's letter, inscribed his own thoughts—namely, Houston's demands would either defeat annexation or lead to a war between Europe and America; besides, Texas' relations with France and England would be complicated and entangled, revolution at home would occur; and Houston might, as he offered no explanation, be planning the defeat of annexation, war, or the breakdown of Jones' own presidential administration, soon to commence, in December 1844.[59e]

But the national presidential campaign of 1844, begun in 1840, was to determine the fate of annexation. In 1840, the Democratic Van Buren had been defeated by Harrison and Tyler and, in 1844, Van Buren, again, was to have been the Democratic nomination. Henry Clay was to be rewarded by the Whigs in 1844 and to succeed Harrison. But Harrison's death and Tyler's succession in 1841 threatened Clay's aspirations while Tyler's raising of the annexation issue conclusively sidetracked Van Buren's nomination and defeated Clay's chance of election. For Clay had, prior to the Whig national convention, declared against immediate annexation and Van Buren, almost contemporaneously, had restated his convictions that, while annexation would not violate the Constitution, he was unwilling to act until Mexico recognized Texan independence and made peace. So, on 1st May 1844, the Whigs nominated Clay but the Democrats switched to the dark horse annexationist, James K. Polk of Tennessee, supported by the old warrior, Andrew Jackson. The Democratic platform linked Oregon and Texas in the cry for reoccupation and reannexation, the American Manifest Destiny mania was fanned, and, in November, Polk was elected. And thus Tyler, long convinced of the desirability of early annexation, and now satisfied of the electorate's desire on that subject, reviewed, in his message to Congress on 3rd December 1844, both his own views and those of the people, recommending that the matter be consummated by a joint resolution.[54a] It was the last of February 1845 before the resolution was passed but President Tyler showed no such delay. On 1st March, merely a few hours before his administration was to end, he signed the bill [74b] and, on 3rd March, he despatched the joint resolution to Texas, urging that the Texas Congress act favourably and immediately.[74c, 73c] Then, anticipating efforts of both British and French diplomats to defeat annexation, Tyler instructed the American minister to Texas, Andrew Jackson Donelson, to induce the Texas government to accept speedily.

Tyler's fears of British and French opposition were well founded. Even in Mexico, already ablaze with the news of the annexation movement in the United States, and still angry over the flag incident, there was speculation of British interference. In January 1845, when the election of Polk had announced popular approval of annexation and while Congress was still debating terms, Aberdeen wrote Elliot:

What may be the result in the United States of these redoubled exertions on the part of the Advocates of Annexation it is impossible with certainty to foresee. Her Majesty's Government hope that the honesty and good sense of a large and influential portion of the Publick in that Country (the United States) may resist the impolicy and danger of committing the conduct of the State, in a matter of such delicacy, to the direction of men so violent and unscrupulous as those who have come forward as the leaders in this cause.[22a]

Furthermore, opined Lord Aberdeen, regarding the attitude of the Texans themselves:

> Her Majesty's Government are firmly convinced that the dignity and prosperity of that country (Texas) are more secure in its own keeping than under the institutions of any other government, however peaceful. . . . It must be long before a newly settled and comparatively thinly peopled country would command the attention and the weight which would make up for an abandonment of the privilege of self-government—if indeed such a result should ever be attainable.[22a]

Mexico, wrote Aberdeen, seemed to be leaning toward recognition of Texan independence and Her Majesty's Government hoped that Mexican recognition would cool Texas' annexation fever. On 15th April 1845, Aberdeen informed Cowley that he gathered from the Bankhead, Pakenham, and Elliot despatches that the Government of Mexico had 'materially moderated their tone and pretension with respect to Texas and the recognition of its independence by Mexico, and that they are anxiously awaiting some demonstration on the part of Great Britain and France' to 'open a negotiation for that recognition.' [22b]

Continuing his lengthy letter, Aberdeen mentioned that:

> The report of Captain Elliot fully corroborates that of Mr. Pakenham on the point of the growing distaste evinced by the Texians to the terms of annexation proposed by the United States' Congress, and gives fair-ground to hope that that feeling may be turned to excellent account in defeating the project of annexation, provided Mexico can be brought at once to acknowledge the independence of Texas.[22c]

Regarding French attitude, 'H.M.'s Govt. assume that the Govt. of France still adhere to the sentiments which they have frequently expressed in favour of the independence of Texas' and that France now as before considered Texas' independence as 'politically expedient and beneficial' and 'likely to conduce not only to the security of Mexico, and the prosperity of Texas, but also to the preservation of general peace.' [22c] As for Mexico, Aberdeen accented that he could not deny 'that little dependence can be placed either on the stability of the present Mexican Government or on the steadiness with which it would be likely to adhere to any line of policy,' with respect to Texas or the United States.[22d] Moreover, Her Majesty's

Government 'would not propose to enter into any guarantee whatever with respect to either of these States,' Mexico or Texas, 'whether to secure inviolability of frontier' or 'protection and succour against encroachment on the part of any other Power,' [22e] for Great Britain 'merely wished to exert all the influence of their moral influence added to that of France' in order 'to secure peace and future security,' both for Mexico and for Texas and 'that not from any feeling of hostility or opposition to the United States' but from 'a sense of friendly consideration for the wellbeing of Mexico and Texas.' [22e] In other words, Great Britain in proposing 'to stand forward at this moment in conjunction with France, in order to secure the independence of Texas,' presented themselves 'as the advocates, not so much of British interests, as of the interests of Mexico and Texas.' [22e] In addition, Aberdeen made it clear that Great Britain would undertake nothing that could involve her in war with the United States for 'Her Majesty's Government . . . do not conceive that they would be justified in exposing Great Britain to the serious risks of a war in seeking to extablish that (Texan) independence.' [22d]

Some pages later in the Foreign Office Records is enclosed the *Draft of A Declaration of Victoria as to an offer to Texas of the joint Mediation of Great Britain and France toward obtaining the Recognition of Texas by Mexico.*[22f] Preceding this entry is a note by Aberdeen to Elliot that Elliot's various despatches [14c] concerning annexation, and 'the one marked secret,' had been received at the Foreign Office and 'laid before the Queen.' [14d]

British Colonial reaction to Texas annexation is interesting. The 25th February 1845 *Bermuda Royal Gazette* quoted the *New York Express Courier* correspondent who, on 31st January previous, had commented:

> Those who are not here in Washington can have but a faint idea of the war spirit that pervaded the majority of the House of Representatives; for it is exhibited more in conversation than in those debates which go before the public. It is not confined to the young, and to the Hotspurs of the West, but pervades the South, and has possessions of grey headed democrats of, what should be the peace loving state of Pennsylvania. They are mad of the British lion, and of a desire for more territory—there is good land in Texas and Oregon, say they, and we must immediately possess it—there are rich mines and fertile fields in Mexico, and they too must be brought within our domination,—and warming with the subject, their appetite growing by what it feeds on they exclaim, 'this whole continent must be ours; our destiny is to carry our laws and our institutions throughout its whole extent.' [1b]

The editor of the *Bermuda Royal Gazette* added his own interpretation and commented that 'to the sober minded reader' the *New York Express* article 'appears as merely a vain and boastful declaration,' but 'it is nevertheless the language of the people's representatives uttered in the legislative halls of the nation, with a manifest determination to carry these visions for the future into practical operation, by a system of grasping acquisition which they have already commenced.' [1b]

Elliot, writing from Galveston early in February 1845, informed London that:

> Upon the whole, incline I to the opinion that there is a growing disposition here (in Texas) to believe that annexation will be very difficult in the United States; a state of feeling which of course encourages the party in favour of Independence, and if the present effort in the United States is defeated, it is probable that there will be a considerable manifestation in Texas against any further entertainment of the subject. [14e]

Continuing his theme, Elliot noted that neither Houston nor Jones publicly favoured annexation, that Houston had advised upon the immediate conclusion of an agreement with Mexico, that Jones in his inaugural address had not expressed his own views as favouring annexation, and that Jones, in his personal conversations with Elliot, had always emphasized the fact that he, the President of the Republic, was but the agent of the people whose will he must execute. Deeply Elliot believed, and so reported to Aberdeen, that the strong men of the Texan government were opposed to annexation and this group, Elliot thought, was really gaining in numbers and in control of the situation. [14e]

Also, from Bankhead in Mexico, Aberdeen received information of Mexico's readiness to concede Texan independence. On 1st March 1845, Bankhead wrote the Foreign Office that, upon the arrival in Mexico of the news of the annexation resolutions, Mexico, finally, became thoroughly aroused and keenly apprehensive. Cuevas, the Mexican minister of foreign affairs, had declared himself ready to present to his Congress the project of Texan independence if he could, at the same time, be assured of British and French approval and support; also, reported Bankhead, Cuevas had proposed to bring up the abolition question again in the treaty with Texas, but Bankhead, reminding Aberdeen of the verbal instructions which the Foreign Secretary gave him in London before he set out for Mexico, evaded reply to Cuevas on the slavery issue. [22g] Much as Bankhead desired to see Mexico take such recognition action, and confident as Cuevas was that the Mexican Congress, if assured of British action, would take such action, Bankhead could not give the desired assurance and replied to Cuevas, cautiously, that 'any assistance from England must be a *moral* one, for that whatever disposition may have at one time existed to go beyond that line, had now been withdrawn.' [22g]

Elliot was not far wrong in his convictions that annexation would fail. On 2nd December 1844, Andrew Jackson wrote Donelson expressing his mounting fear that Texas might become 'worse than a colony of England, involved in constant conflict with the United States.' If Texas remained independent, the Old Warrior was convinced that she would be 'a province of England.'[37a] The previous August, Calhoun had written to Donelson lamenting British activities in Texas and using the terms 'Texas (had been) invaded' and 'British gold' was there.[37b] Then, on 20th December, a few weeks after Jackson had warned Donelson, Duff Green, writing from Washington-on-the-Beazos, informed Donelson that 'Capt. Elliot arrived here last night. He promises that in case Texas will pledge herself against annexation England will obtain the consent of Mexico for her Independence.' Concluding his letter to Donelson, Green expressed his own fear that the United States 'may offer Texas annexation on terms she will not accept, and that (the) matter will become mixed up with (the) nullification issue.'[37c] Green urged haste and reiterated his long established conviction that Santa Anna would rather see Britain than the United States have Texas.[34a] Not only Texas concerned Green; almost at the same time, he was fearful of British interests and activities on the Pacific and warned that Britain must be kept out of California and Oregon.[39a] On 8th January 1845, Calhoun informed Donelson that he was fearful of the fate of the annexation measure in Congress.[37d] Three months later, on 4th April 1845, Donelson wrote his wife that both the British and French ministers at Galveston were active and that he knew of their 'intrigues.'[37e] Several days later, Donelson wrote that he was beginning to 'see the end of the Texas question. It is safe . . . Houston has disappointed me, and has not given the matter the support I expected.'[37f] On 6th May, Polk's postscript informed Donelson that, in his own opinion, Great Britain intended 'in truth and in fact' to make Texas 'a dependency of her own'[37g] and, several weeks later, Calhoun inquired of Donelson regarding current 'British and French influence' in Texas.[37h] One Eastland assured Donelson that 'the British minister, Captain Charles Elliot,' in preventing annexation, 'works well in harness but can't carry this load.'[37i] President Polk, on the other hand, in a note of 15th June, and which he marked confidential, spoke of Elliot's cleverness and of the 'open intermeddling' of the British chargé.[37j] Polk felt as Calhoun did who, in commissioning Donelson as chargé to Texas, had instructed Donelson that it was his mission 'to patch things up', for the United States Government felt that Texan disappointment 'may be seized upon by an interested and wily diplomacy' and, of all possible consequences, a Texan alliance with Britain 'would be the most disastrous.' [37k] The year previous, Murphy, chargé in Texas, had been warned of British activities in the Republic and, after examining affairs there, had written his government that there was little doubt that Britain was, certainly by 1843, exerting pressure on Texas to acknowledge Mexico's sovereignty, in return for a separate legislature and 'quasi-independence'; and that, while there was then no 'sufficient reason to suppose that England desires to acquire it', it was, nevertheless and most certainly, a subject of deepest interest to the United States.[40a]

Apparently, the slavery issue, that is abolitionist sentiment, was the chief obstacle to annexation, rather than opposition to territorial expansion.[59b] Yet, 'of conscious purpose to aid the Texans in order to bring more slavery territory into the United States' Barker has found no evidence.[61a] The only reference to the subject noticed by this author appears in *The Mississippian* (Jackson) of 18th March 1836, in which a writer, in reviewing a pamphlet by W. H. Wharton on the causes of the Texas Revolution, points out that the possession of Texas by the United States would open an immense region for the diffusing of slaves in which the older slave states could dispose of their surplus to advantage.[61a] In 1836, at the close of the Texas Revolution, Benjamin Lundy's pamphlet title stated what was to become the 'authorized version' [60a] of the motives behind the settlement, revolt, and annexation of Texas:

> The war in Texas; a review of facts and circumstances, showing that this contest is the result of a long premeditated crusade against the government set on foot by slaveholders, land speculators, etc., with the view of re-establishing, extending and perpetuating the system of slavery and the slave trade in the Republic of Mexico.[51]

This pamphlet furnished material for John Quincy Adam's fiery speeches against the slave power as well as a fodder mine in which complacent historians were, for several generations succeeding, to quarry, both uncritically and shallowly. Lundy's argument was so plausible—after 1820, both north and west of Missouri lay vast and beckoning territories from which either free or slave states could multiply their respective numbers; sometime in 1821, the Anglo-American movement into Texas, largely directly from the slave states, began; once in Texas, the emigrants evaded every Mexican attempt to exclude slavery from Texas, its northernmost province; soon, these Texans declared independence of Mexico and fought and won a revolution; then, they set up a Republic and wrote up for it a revolutionary constitution which guaranteed slavery and permitted slave importation from the United States; moreover, for the revolution, the Texans drew strength from Southern slaveholders and Northern land speculators and even President Jackson, a slaveowner himself, had violated neutrality by permitting a military occupation of Mexican territory; then, at their first general election, at which even newly arrived volunteers from the United States voted, the Texans voted almost unanimously for annexation; and the United States not only recognized the infant Republic but was, after a few years of 'hypocritical hesitation,' actually to annex these slavers who proudly called themselves Texans.[60a]

Throughout the post-revolutionary years, this sentiment thrived. By 1840-42, the abolitionist question, much to the disgust of the South:

> . . . had intermittently reappeared in Congress (South Carolina) in the forms of petitions and debates on their receipt, yet no very definite issue had been drawn. As Texas became more and more involved with Mexico, however, South Carolina began to express sympathy for Texas to the extent of sending financial aid, raised through voluntary subscriptions, and, by 1843, it was clear that the abolitionist question was very likely to become really vital in the case of Texas.[63a]

The South Carolina legislature of 1843, 'urged by the belief that England was about to guarantee independence to Texas, on condition of abolition, passed resolutions that steps should be taken by the United States for the annexation of Texas.'[63a]

Elsewhere than from South Carolina came expressions. In April 1842, Archibald Linn, Congressman from New York, offered in the House a motion to strike from an appropriation bill the salary of the minister of Mexico. In his ensuing speech, he declared that 'recent events have satisfied me that new and serious attempts will be made to accomplish the annexation of Texas', an event which Linn maintained he could regard 'only as the annexation of a wen to an otherwise sound body'.[59b] Furthermore, he reminded Congress that annexation would cause war with Mexico, and England, for commercial and other reasons, would join Mexico.[59b] In September of the same year, 1842, John Quincy Adams, from Braintree, Massachusetts, had repeated many of his fiery assertions that he had made in his long harangue during June-July of 1838 and warned his constituents that annexation, as in 1838, was, in 1842, again an issue. As Adams drew the picture, the colonists moved into Texas to wrest it from Mexico; they revolted because Mexico refused to abolish slavery; and, forthwith, the Southern states were striving for annexation in order to win new territory to be divided into more slave states.[45, 52] The next year, in March 1843, Adams and a group of other Washington congressmen issued an address to 'The People of the Free States of the Union.' While admitting that slavery was not the only question involved in annexation, these abolitionists insisted that it was the most important issue and declared that the South's object was to add new weight to her lever's end. 'They said, in effect, that annexation would be unconstitutional and would justify dissolution of the Union by the free states.' [59c] The Indiana, Massachusetts, and other Northern legislatures hastily replied as emphatically opposed to annexation while the Alabama, Mississippi, Tennessee, and other Southern legislatures were equally as emphatic in their resolutions which argued not only the right of the United States to annex Texas but proclaimed annexation indispensable in order to prevent England from gaining control of the province and using it as a base from which to work against slavery in the United States.

In the early spring of 1845, Elliot, convinced that Texas was against annexation, was fortified in this belief when he received Aberdeen's letter of 23rd January 1845.[22a] The attitude of the British government was plain: Polk's election had indicated American popular approval of annexation, Congress even yet was debating terms, and Britain was firmly convinced that only in independence could Texas secure her dignity and prosperity. Furthermore, continued Lord Aberdeen, the President of Mexico seemed to be leaning toward recognition of Texan independence and surely such recognition would make the Texans less anxious for annexation. In January, Elliot had forwarded to the Foreign Office clippings from the Galveston and Houston newspapers which quoted the resolution passed by the Committee on the State of the Republic in the House of Representatives on 29th January. If the United States continued 'to delay indefinitely' annexation and, thereby, 'impair the confidences' of the peoples of both countries, and, perhaps, 'defeat the establishment of relations with other powers', the Committee resolved that 'the President be requested to re-open negotiations for a *permanent* peace with Mexico on the basis of our proper limits to the Rio Bravo del Norte.' [14f]

Certainly Elliot had foundation for his belief that several foremost Texans were only biding their time for a propitious opportunity to declare themselves against annexation. President Jones, Elliot reasoned, sincerely desired the maintenance of independence but would be destitute against popular demand unless he could offer, as an alternative to annexation, recognition of independence by Mexico. On 22nd March, from Galveston, Elliot wrote Aberdeen that the 'intelligence of the success of the annexation measures in the United States arrived here two days since, and with the language of the new President in his inaugural address have certainly given some encouragement to the party favourable to the scheme.,[14g] The supreme necessity for Texas, Elliot informed Aberdeen, was an immediate offer from

Mexico of independence.[14g] And, in quest of such an offer, Elliot determined, if necessary, to go to Mexico.

In April, Elliot received news from Bankhead that Mexico was intensely interested in Ashbel Smith's return to Texas from his European post to become secretary of state under Jones, and in the possible result of his efforts there. Bankhead was convinced that, if the Texan government was sincere in its desire for Mexican recognition, Mexico would acquiesce.[24a] Meanwhile, on 6th April, William Shannon, Minister of the United States, writing the Secretary of State, was fearful of renewed British efforts to induce Texas not to accept annexation.[34b] The year before, on 2nd February 1844, Waddy Thompson had informed the Washington government that Mexico would not like to have Texas annexed by Britain[34c] but, on 15th June following, Green was to write Washington that he believed that Santa Anna would rather see Britain than the United States have Texas.[34d] Elliot had already been sought by Smith for conferences in which the new secretary of state affirmed his countrymen's growing anti-annexation sentiment and described local conditions as he desired Elliot to report them to Aberdeen. Smith suggested that Texas would voluntarily pledge herself never to be annexed to any other country, provided Mexico promptly recognized her independence and England consented to act as arbiter in any boundary dispute between Texas and Mexico. Elliot faithfully reported all these conferences to the Foreign Office but, remembering previous undirection by the Foreign Office in his China mission, and the painful reprimand that followed his desperate and independent action in China, Elliot refused to express himself to Smith. But, to the Foreign Office, he did express his strong opposition to a British boundary guarantee.[14h]

In January of 1845, the London office sent out the joint instructions of Great Britain and France and, on 24th March, they were in Elliot's hands. Mindful of Donelson's activities to fan the annexation fever, cognizant of the vote in the American Senate authorizing a direct offer to Texas, and seizing advantage of Donelson's absence from the Republic, Elliot told Saligny that he believed that Donelson would soon return from New Orleans completely commissioned to conclude annexation formalities with all haste. Together, Elliot and Saligny hastened to Washington-on-the-Brazos to prevent, if possible, any immediate Texan acceptance of proposals from the United States. The two chargés in a series of interviews with President Jones, Secretary of State Smith, and others of the Republic's cabinet were told that, frankly, these men desired independence but realized their first duty was to execute the will of the country, which clamoured for annexation. All they could do then was to delay decision, thus affording opportunity for acceptance of some other solution than annexation. And, in this promise of delay, Elliot found much encouragement and reported to Aberdeen that delay itself might, eventually, end in a defeat of American policy. On 29th March 1845, the ultimatum-memorandum, signed by Jones, Smith, Saligny, and Elliot, was completed, Elliot and Saligny giving their personal pledges that it should be known only to the courts of London and Paris, to their ministries in Washington, D.C., and to the Mexican government. In order to carry out the plan proposed in this document, Elliot urged Jones to send Smith to Europe and, at the same time, Elliot himself offered to take the document to Mexico secretly and to use his personal influence with the government there.[14i] The Texan ultimatum proposed: (1) Mexico consents to acknowledge the independence of Texas, (2) Texas engages that she will stipulate in the treaty not to annex herself or become subject to any country whatever, (3) limits the other conditions to be matters of arrangement in the final treaty, and (4) Texas will be willing to remit disputed points respecting territory and other matters to the arbitration of umpires.[14i]

In March 1845, the high priests of diplomacy were alarmed. Secretary of State Buchanan, in charging Charles A. Wickliffe 'as secret agent to help Donelson' in the annexation fight, wrote much about the 'machinations' of both British and French in Texas and said both those nations were working 'in concert' through their ministers to Texas.[38a] To Thomas A. Larkin, United States consul in Monterey, Buchanan mentioned the possibility of a transfer of California to Britain.[38b] At the same time, Edward Everett in London was confidentially reporting to Buchanan the current local rumours of the possible Californian cession to Britain, adding his proposal that California be ceded to Russia.[36a] From Texas, Donelson informed the secretary of state that 'foreign influence against annexation', certainly that of Britain and Ashbel Smith, was alarming.[37l]

Elliot, actuated by zeal in a cause, convinced that his mission which occasioned it must be kept completely secret, so that no suspicion might be aroused in the public minds as to what was afoot, and especially desirous that the government of the United States should remain ignorant of British interference in annexation, announced a journey to Charleston, South Carolina, and sailed out of Galveston harbour on H.M.S. *Electra*. Out of sight of land, he transferred to the British ship *Eurydice*, under Captain George Elliot, on the North American and West Indian station.[XVIII, 79a] The *Eurydice* was bound for Vera Cruz from which port her Captain

---

xviii Captain George Elliot was the eldest son of Rear-Admiral Hon. George Elliot, C.B., second son of Gilbert, first Earl of Minto.

proceeded overland to the City of Mexico ostensibly to carry British despatches to Bankhead. Charles Elliot, concealing his precious documents, accompanied his cousin incognito.[58i] On 19th April 1845, William S. Parrott wrote Secretary of State Buchanan from Vera Cruz of 'Capt. Elliot, the British agent, being robbed on the road to Mexico.'[34e]

The Herrera government was inclined to peace, but the events of 1845, unhappily, lent themselves to political incendiarism. In March, when the United States offered annexation to Texas, the Mexican minister withdrew from Washington and diplomatic relations were severed. In April, Elliot arrived in Mexico with terms offered by Texas herself, namely, recognition of Texan independence on condition that Texas should maintain its independence. The Mexican cabinet listened intently to the proposal and to Elliot's powerful arguments that it be accepted immediately and without alteration. But it was only after long delay that Cuevas, the Mexican minister of foreign affairs, signed. On 17th May, Bankhead delivered to Elliot the Mexican Congress' belated and conditional offer of recognition to Texas—in addition to accepting the Texan proposals, Mexico stipulated that its reply should be null and void if Texas accepted annexation.[76a, 53a] Both Bankhead and Elliot were relieved but gravely anxious because of the long lapse of time occasioned by the Mexican's dilatory habits.

Meanwhile, Donelson was alarmed at 'the report of a British fleet entering the Gulf' and, on 11th May, reported this rumour to his government in the United States.[35a] Ten days later, he wrote of Elliot's 'mediation' between Texas and Mexico and recommended that the United States be prepared for war with Mexico.[35b] On 23rd May, Elliot hastily set out upon his return journey to Texas, boarded a French warship at Vera Cruz, and reported his arrival at Galveston to his home government on 30th May. He hurried to Washington-on-the-Brazos, delivered the Mexican document, and heard, with great disappointment, President Jones' disquieting opinion that now the popular annexation fever made its acceptance doubtful. On 2nd June, Donelson having arrived at Galveston from New Orleans, detailed for Buchanan, the 'terms of his (Elliot's) mediation and efforts to defeat annexation'. [35c]

On 6th June, President Jones wrote Elliot a note, marked private, which asked Elliot's opinion to the query 'Would it not be well that Mexico should make a *formal* declaration of a cessation of hostilities on her part?' [14j] At the same time, Jones declared peace with Mexico in accordance with the documents Elliot had secured in Mexico for Texas and, soon thereafter, Jones summoned a convention to consider both the Mexican proposals and the American offer. Elliot was, by now, completely disillusioned—annexation, he thought, was a foregone conclusion. Furthermore, his recent clandestine activities in Mexico, and even his very presence in the Republic, were arousing more and more suspicion and, consequently, only aiding the annexationists' cause. So his departure seeming advisable, and having received Aberdeen's instructions of 3rd May, with the plan of a document to be signed by himself, Saligny, and the Texan authorities, Elliot, despondent and convinced that both he and British policy had failed in Texas, departed for New York, where he hoped a change of climate would alleviate an attack of fever which, recurrently, had plagued him throughout his years in Texas.[14k] Travelling eastward, he, now known as 'the man in the white hat,' stopped over in New Orleans and, almost daily, sent Aberdeen alarming annexationist clippings from the Louisiana newspapers.[14k] On 28th July, he had reached New York and, with a bitter pen, informed the London office that he was 'fearing that slavery might again be introduced into the ceded territory of Texas' and 'thus incur for Mexico the certainty of constant frontier dispute and raids arising out of the escape of slaves, and the other worse evil of filling these lands with settlers of the same kind as those who have already proved so dangerous to Mexico'.[14l]

Meanwhile, in England, there had been a loud chorus of approval and rejoicing over the proposed mission to Mexico, and Elliot had been praised by Aberdeen who wrote Bankhead that Her Majesty's Government was enthusiastic and appreciative of the 'dexterity and activity' of her agent in Texas and that both England and France had undoubtedly gained an advantage in checking the successful progress of the Annexation Project'.[58j]

Continuing to express British official support of Elliot's enterprise, Lord Aberdeen wrote Bankhead that, if Mexico still stubbornly refused to accept British advice, Great Britain and France would wash their hands of the matter, and would 'consider themselves entirely absolved from all further interference in the affairs of Mexico with reference to the United States'.[58j] Moreover, the friendly relations of England and the United States had been injured by President Polk's inaugural address which stated that the United States would concede none of Britain's contentions as to Oregon. For a while, war itself seemed possible and England, vexed and rebuffed by Polk's arrogance, may easily have been the more enthusiastic with the announcement of Elliot's proposed mission to Mexico. Then came the Mexican's tantalizing delays which the Foreign Office interpreted as failure.

Daily, Aberdeen felt more keenly the utter hopelessness of defeating the land-hungry United States and, all along, he resented the cloak-and-dagger technique employed by Elliot. For this, the Foreign Secretary reproved Elliot, reminding him that it laid Britain open to charges of intriguing in

Texas; in truth, British diplomacy prided itself on its open and frank methods. Besides this comment on the Mexican mission, Aberdeen elaborated for Elliot, in a despatch dated 3rd July 1845, upon general British policy in America. The constant object of that policy was to maintain peace on the North American continent. Aberdeen believed that only in peace could British interests be secured; that, while Great Britain need not fear United States aggression upon Canada, yet the steady United States aggression portended only evil; and, Aberdeen predicted, as a result of the United States' insatiable land hunger, civil war which might or would involve British interests. Concluding his despatch to Elliot, Aberdeen, though commending the fertility, invention and energy that inspired the enterprise, informed Elliot that he had elaborated for his benefit British general policy in North America 'to demonstrate to you that the mystery which you unfortunately threw around your recent proceedings was not only unnecessary, but liable to be misconstrued in such a manner as to make our policy appear in a light the very reverse of that which it ought to bear'. [22h]

Late in June, Mexico heard of Jones' proclamation and of the calling of the convention and, in spite of assurances and peace demands from Bankhead, Cuevas threatened war. Early in July, the Texas convention convened, rejected peace with Mexico upon the basis of independence and, on the anniversary of American colonial independence, 4th July, committed Texas to annexation, the formal change of sovereignty being deferred until February 1846. In England, the July 1845 vote of the Texas convention was regarded as finally and irrevocably settling the Texas question. Elliot was ordered to return from the United States to his post in Texas, reproved, and explicitly directed to stay in Texas and maintain his position there as a representative of the dignity of the British nation, until the country should become a corporate part of the United States.

Welcome relief to the annexation furor were Aberdeen's orders to Elliot, in the closing weeks of 1845, to aid the Earl of Lincoln in Her Britannic Majesty's Government's efforts and project to enlarge and enrich the Royal Botanical Gardens at Kew 'by procuring Seeds and Roots, and new or rare or useful Plants, etc., from Foreign sources, through means which may be within the reach of Her Majesty's Representatives abroad'. [22i]

But Elliot was disinclined to aid Lincoln in his scientific pursuits. In the last days of his Texas mission, he was more occupied in meeting the American attacks occasioned by his secret mission and with his own defence before Aberdeen than he was with even England's dignity, the

Republic of Texas' affairs, much less with horticulture. The Buchanan-Donelson letters, which appeared in the *New York Herald* in December of 1845, talked of his 'secrecy' and distressed Elliot, who forwarded voluminous clippings to the Foreign Office. He was informed that, when the formalities of annexation were concluded, he was to close his office, bring with him all the records of that office, and return to England. Thus, Elliot, convinced of the ill bodings of annexation for Texas and mindful of Aberdeen's prophecy of disintegration of the Union as well, accepted the inevitable and returned to England.

BIBLIOGRAPHY & REFERENCES

MICROFILM

1 C.O.R. 41/2. Newspapers, 1844–47, *Royal Gazette* and *Bermuda Commercial and General Advertiser and Recorder.*
 a p.10; b p.119.

2 F.O.R. 75/1. Texas. 1840. General Hamilton.

3 F.O.R. 75/2. Texas. 1841. General Hamilton and Mr Kennedy.
 a p.7.

4 F.O.R. 75/3. Texas. Aug.-Dec. 1842. Consuls Elliot and Kennedy, Foreign various and Consular Domestic.
 a p.1; b pp.83-131; c p.132; d p.13; e p.15ff; f p.17; g p.21; h p.146; i pp.38,44; j p.48; k p.58; l p.55ff; m p.63; n p.71; o p.73.

5 F.O.R. 75/4. Texas. 1842. Captain Elliot, Diplomatic.
 a p.3; b pp.105-112; c pp.68-73; d p.44; e p.52; f p.80; g p.32; h pp.15-21; i p.51; j pp.118-126,128-131, 142-147,158-160,161-164; k pp.99-104; l p.100; m p.101; n p.102; o p.103; p p.188ff; q Elliot to Addington, 16.12.1842.

6 F.O.R. 75/5. Texas. 1842. Mr Smith, and various.

7 F.O.R. 75/6. Texas. 1843. Captain Elliot, Diplomatic.
 a Elliot to Aberdeen, 28.1.1843; b Houston to Elliot, 24.1.1843; c Elliot to Addington, 26.3.1843; d Aberdeen to Elliot, 18.5.1843; e Aberdeen to Elliot, 3.6.1843; f Elliot to Pakenham, 14.4.1843; g Elliot to Aberdeen, 8.6.1843; h Elliot to Doyle, 21.6.1843; i Elliot to Jones, 24.7.1843; j Elliot to Aberdeen, 30.9.1843; k Elliot to Doyle, 10.10.1843; l Elliot to Aberdeen, 31.10.1843; m Elliot to Aberdeen, 31.12.1843.

8 F.O.R. 75/7. Texas. 1843. Consuls Captain Elliot, Mr Kennedy, and Consular Domestic.

9 F.O.R. 75/8. Texas. 1843. Domestic. Mr A. Smith, and various.
 a Smith to Aberdeen, 1.8.1843; b Aberdeen to Smith, 11.9.1843.

10 F.O.R. 75/9. Texas. 1844. Captain Elliot, Diplomatic and Consular.
 a Elliot to Aberdeen, 15.1.1844; b Elliot to Aberdeen, 17.2.1844.

11 F.O.R. 75/10. Texas. 1844. Consuls Kennedy, McDougall, Foreign various and Consular Domestic.

12 F.O.R. 75/11. Texas. 1844. Domestic, Mr Ashbel Smith, Mr Rate, and various.

13 F.O.R. 75/12. Texas. 1845. To Captain Elliot, Diplomatic.

14 F.O.R. 75/13. Texas. 1845. From Captain Elliot.
 a p.43; b p.7ff; c pp.11-26; d p.76; e p.33; f p.41; g p.105; h Elliot to Aberdeen, 6.3.1845; i Elliot to Aberdeen, 2.4.1845; j p.151ff; k p.155; l p.170.

15 F.O.R. 75/14. Texas. 1845. Consuls Elliot, Kennedy, Foreign various and Consular Domestic.

16 F.O.R. 75/15. Texas. 1845. Domestic, Mr Terrell, Mr A. Smith, and various.

17 F.O.R. 75/16. Texas. 1846. Jan.-June. Captain Elliot, Diplomatic.

18 F.O.R. 75/17. Texas. 1846. Consuls Elliot, Kennedy, Lynn, Consular Domestic.

19 F.O.R. 75/18. Texas. 1842. Captain Elliot, Diplomatic and Consular, Archives.

20 F.O.R. 75/19. Texas. 1843. Captain Elliot, Diplomatic and Consular, Archives.

21 F.O.R. 75/20. Texas. 1844. Captain Elliot, Diplomatic and Consular, Archives.
   a p.39; *b* p.445; *c* p.77ff; *d* pp.3-10; *e* pp.12-36; *f* Cowley to Aberdeen, 15.1.1844.

22 F.O.R. 75/21. Texas. 1845. Captain Elliot, Diplomatic and Consular, Archives.
   a p.2; *b* p.52; *c* p.53; *d* p.54; *e* p.55; *f* p.74; *g* p.8ff; *h* Aberdeen to Elliot, 3.7.1845; *i* p.107.

23 F.O.R. 75/22. Texas. 1842–45. Captain Elliot, Correspondence with the Texan Government Archives.

24 F.O.R. 75/23. Texas. 1842–45. Captain Elliot, Correspondence with the British Mission in Mexico, Archives.
   a Bankhead to Elliot, 8.4.1845.

25 F.O.R. 84/374. Slave Trade. 1841. Mexico, Hayti, Texas, New Granada, Venezuela, Central America, Ecuador.
   a pp.1841,84-420.

26 F.O.R. 84/420. Slave Trade. 1842. Mexico, Texas, Venezuela, Hayti.

27 F.O.R. 84/479. Slave Trade. 1843. Hayti: Consul Ussher. Texas: Domestic (Mr Ashbel Smith), Consular (Mr Kennedy).
   a Aberdeen to Elliot, 30.4.1843; *b* Aberdeen to Elliot, 30.5.1843; *c* Elliot to Aberdeen, 25.7.1843; *d* Canning to Elliot, 27.10.1843; *e* Aberdeen to Elliot, Nov. 1843.

28 F.O.R. 84/532. Slave Trade. 1844. Hanse Towns: Colonel Hodges, and Domestic. Hayti: Mr Ussher Texas: Captain Elliot and Mr Kennedy, Domestic, Mr A. Smith.

29 F.O.R. 84/590. Slave Trade. 1845. Hanse Towns: Foreign, and Domestic. Hayti: Texas: Foreign and Consular (Galveston).

30 F.O.R. 84/646. Slave Trade. 1846. United States of America: Mr Pakenham, Mr McLane, Mr Bancroft, Consular, Baltimore, Boston, Charleston, Galveston, Mobile, New Orleans, New York, Norfolk, Philadelphia, Portland, Savannah.

31 F.O.R. 94/365. Texas. Ratification of Treaties. 1840, 13th Nov., 1841, 6th Feb. Treaty of commerce and navigation.

32 F.O.R. 94/365. Texas. Ratification of Treaties. 1840, 14th Nov., 1841, 6th Feb. Additional convention to the foregoing.

33 F.O.R. 94/366. Texas. Ratification of Treaties. 1840, 16th Nov., 1842, 24th Jan. Treaty for the suppression of the slave trade.

MANUSCRIPTS

34 Despatches from U.S. Ministers to Mexico, Vol. 29. National Archives, Department of State Archives, Washington, D.C.
   a Duff Green to Secretary of State, 15.6.1844; *b* Shannon to Secretary of State, 6.4.1845; *c* Thompson to Secretary of State, 2.2.1844; *d* Green to Secretary of State, 15.6.1844; *e* Parrott to Buchanan, 19.4.1845.

35 Despatches from Ministers of U.S. to Texas. Vol. 50. National Archives, Washington, D.C.
   a Donelson to Secretary of State, 11.5.1845; *b* Donelson to Secretary of State, 22.5.1845; *c* Donelson to Secretary of State, 2.6.1845.

36 Despatches from U.S. Ministers, Ministers to Britain. Vol. 53, No. 284. National Archives, Department of State Archives, Washington, D.C.
   a Everett to Buchanan, 28.3.1845.

37 Andrew J. Donelson Papers. Vol. 9, 1840–44; Vol. 10, 1844–45. Manuscripts Division, Library of Congress, Washington, D.C.
   Vol. 9: *k* Calhoun to Donelson, 18.6.1844.
   Vol. 10: *a* Andrew Jackson to Donelson, 2.12.1844; *b* Calhoun to Donelson, 26.8.1844; *c* Duff Green to Donelson, 20.12.1844; *d* Calhoun to Donelson, 9.1.1845; *e* Donelson to Elizabeth, 5.4.1845; *f* Donelson to Elizabeth, 16.4.1844; *g* Polk to Donelson, 6.5.1845; *h* Calhoun to Donelson, 23.5.1845; *i* Eastland to Donelson, 21.5.1845; *j* Polk to Donelson, 15.6.1845; *l* Donelson to Secretary of State, 29.4.1845.

38 General Records of the Department of State. Group No. 59, Special Missions, Vol. 7. National Archives, Washington, D.C.
   a p.213ff; *b* p.230ff.

39 Duff Green Letters. Manuscripts Division, Library of Congress, Washington, D.C.
   a Duff Green to Crallé, 28.10.1844.

40 State Department Instructions. Mexico, Vol. 15, 29th May, 1833-29th March, 1845. National Archives, Washington, D.C.
   a item 53, pp.268-73.

CHARLES ELLIOT R.N.

41 Letters (1950): R. A. McLemore, Professor, Mississippi Southern College, Hattiesburgh, Mississippi, to Clagette Blake.

42 Letters of Ashbel Smith to Sam Houston. Archives, The University of Texas.
   a Two letters, 3.10.1842; *b* Letter, 21.10.1842; *c* Letter, 30.12.1842; *d* Letter, 1.2.1843; *e* Letter, 11.4.1843; *f* Letter 1.8.1843; *g* Letter, 30.10.1843; *h* Letter, 27.11.1843; *i* Letter, 2.6.1844; *j* Letter, 7.4.1845; *k* Letter, 25.3.1848; *l* Letter, 9.5.1851,

43 Papers of Ashbel Smith, Archives, The University of Texas.

44 Special Missions. Vol. 7, dated 15th, December 1823, General Records of the Department of State, Group No. 59. National Archives, Washington, D.C.

PRINTED

45 Adams, Charles Francis (ed.), *Memoirs of John Quincy Adams* Philadelphia: J. B. Lippincott and Company, 1874–77.

46 Adams, Ephraim Douglass (ed.), *British Diplomatic Correspondence Concerning the Republic of Texas*, 1836–1846. Austin n.d., Reprinted from *The Texas State Historical Association Quarterly*, and *The Southwestern Historical Quarterly*, Vols. XVI to XXI.
   a pp.52-60.

47 Gammel, Hans Peter Nielsen (comp.), *The Laws of Texas*, 1822–1897. Vol. II .Austin: The Gammel Book Company, 1898.
   a p.661; *b* pp.905–912; *c* pp.880-888.

48 Garrison, George P. (ed.), *The Diplomatic Correspondence of The Republic of Texas*. 3 vols. American Historical Association, *Annual Reports* for 1907 and 1908. Washington, D.C.: Government Printing Office, 1908–09.
   Vol. I: *a* p.201.
   Vol. II: *c* p.766; *d* p.792.
   Vol. III. *b* p.945, *e* p.943, pp.1474-76, 1524-27, 1537-40, 1543-48, 1557-60, 1570-73; *f* pp.1548-53, 1474-76, 1537-40, 1557-60, 1570-73, 1553-54, 1563-69; *g* p.907; *h* p.917; *i* p.939; *j* p.996; *k* p.1009 *l* p.1356; *m* pp.1485-88.

49 Hansard, *Parliamentary Debates*. 3rd Ser. Vols. XXV, XXXIV and LXXI. London: Thomas Curson Hansard, 1836 and 1843.
   a Vol. XXXIV, p.1107; *b* Vol. XXV, pp.928-942; *c* Vol. LXXI, p.917.

50 H.R. Ex. Doc. No. 271. 28th Cong., 1st Sess.

51 Lundy, Benjamin, *The War in Texas; a review of facts and circumstances, showing that this contest is the result of a long premeditated crusade against the government set on foot by slaveholders, land speculators, etc., with the view of re-establishing, extending and perpetuating the system of slavery and the slave trade in the Republic of Mexico*. Philadelphia: Merrihew and Gunn, 1836.

52 Nevins, Allan (ed.), *The Diary of John Quincy Adams*. New York, London: Longmans, Green and Company, 1929.

53 Ramsey, Albert C. (ed.), *The Other Side: or Notes for the History of the War between Mexico and the United States*. New York, 1850.
   a p.27.

54 Richardson, James D. (ed.), *A Compilation of the Messages and Papers of the Presidents, 1789–1897*. 10 vols. Washington, D.C.: Government Printing Office, 1896–99.
   a III, p.2195ff.

55 *Sessional Papers*. 1847. Commons, Vol. 64. London: H.M. Stationery Office.

56 Williams, Amelia W., and Barker, Eugene C. (eds.), *The Writings of Sam Houston*, 1813–1863. 8 vols Austin: The University of Texas Press, 1938.

57 Winkler, Ernest William (ed.), *Secret Journals of the Senate, Republic of Texas*, 1836–1845. Austin, Texas Library and Historical Commission, *First Biennial Report*, 1911.
   a p.198; *b* p.221.

58 Adams, Ephraim Douglass, *British Interests and Activities in Texas*, 1838–1846. Baltimore: The Johns Hopkins Press, 1910.
   a p.15; *b* p.79ff; *c* p.52; *d* p.123; *e* p.130; *f* p.136; *g* p.137; *h* pp.152-54; *i* p.211; *j* p.219.

59 Barker, Eugene C., 'The Annexation of Texas', reprinted from *The Southwestern Historical Quarterly*, Vol. L, No. 1, July 1946.
   a p.13; *b* p.14; *c* p.15; *d* p.16; *e* p.20.

60 Barker, Eugene C., 'The Influence of Slavery in the Colonization of Texas', *The Mississippi Valley Historical Review*, Vol. XI, No. 1, June 1924. The Mississippi Valley Historical Association.
   a p.3ff.

61 Barker, Eugene C., 'The United States and Mexico, 1835–1837', *The Mississippi Valley Historical Review*, Vol. I, No. 1, June 1914. The Mississippi Valley Historical Association.
   a p.9.

62 Binkley, W. C., *The Expansionist Movement in Texas*, 1836–1850. Berkeley: The University of California Press, 1925.
   a p.28.

63 Boucher, Chauncey S., 'The Annexation of Texas and The Bluffton Movement in South Carolina', *The Mississippi Valley Historical Review*, Vol. VI, No. 1, June 1919. The Mississippi Valley Historical Association.
   a p.13.

64 Buckingham, James Silk, *The Slave States of America*. 2 vols. London, Paris: Fisher, Son and Company, 1842.

65 Chase, Mary Catherine, *Négociations de la République du Texas en Europe*, 1837–1845. Paris: Librairie Ancienne Honoré Champion, 1932.
   a pp.67, 87; *b* pp.153-55; *c* pp.119-143.

66 Dienst, Alex, 'The Navy of the Republic of Texas', *The Quarterly of the Texas State Historical Association*, Vol. XIII, No. 1. July 1909. Austin: The Texas State Historical Association, 1910.
   a p.30.

67 Garrison, George P., *Texas: A Contest of Civilizations*. Boston and New York: Houghton Mifflin Company, 1903.
   a p.241.

68 Hill, Jim Dan, *The Texas Navy in Forgotten Battles and Shirtsleeve Diplomacy*. Chicago: The University of Chicago Press, 1937.
   a p.144.

69 Kennedy, William, *Texas: The Rise, Progress, and Prospects of the Republic of Texas*. 2 vols. London: 1841.

70 Latané, John Holladay, *A History of American Foreign Policy*. Garden City, New York: Doubleday, Doran and Company, 1928.
   a p.248.

71 McLemore, R. A., 'The Influence of French Diplomatic Policy on the Annexation of Texas', *The Southwestern Historical Quarterly*, Vol. XLIII, No. 3. January 1940. Austin: The Texas State Historical Association. (Professor McLemore, of Mississippi Southern College, Hattiesburg, here summarized his findings from materials in the French Foreign Office.)

72 *Niles Weekly Register*. Baltimore, Washington, and Philadelphia, 1811–1849.
   a 10.6.1843.

73 Reeves, Jesse Siddall, *American Diplomacy under Tyler and Polk*. Baltimore: The Johns Hopkins Press 1907.
   a p.119; *b* p.133; *c* p.185.

74 Rives, George Lockhart, *The United States and Mexico*, 1821–1848, Vol. I. 2 vols. New York: C. Scribner's Sons, 1913.
   a p.636; *b* p.689; *c* pp.690-93.

75 Smith, Ashbel, *Reminiscences of the Texas Republic*. Galveston, 1876.
   a p.61ff.

76 Smith, Justin Harvey, *The Annexation of Texas*. New York: Barnes and Noble, Inc., 1941.
   a pp.430, 456.

77 Smither, Harriet, 'English Abolitionism and the Annexation of Texas', *The Southwestern Historical Quarterly*, XXXII, No. 1. July 1928. Austin: The Texas State Historical Association.

78 Worley, J. L., 'The Diplomatic Relations of England and the Republic of Texas', *The Quarterly of the Texas State Historical Association*, Vol. IX, No. 1. July 1905. Austin: The Texas State Historical Association, 1906.
   a pp.1-40; *b* p.15.

79 O'Byrne's *Naval Biographical Dictionary*.
   a p 333.

NEWSPAPERS

80 *Austin City Gazette*.
   a 22.12.1841, Report of Finance Committee relative to the Recall of the Loan Commissions.

81 *Telegraph and Texas Register*.
   a 13.1.1841.

VI

Gilded Exile

THE remainder of Charles Elliot's story amounted to exile, but gilded exile. After Texas, he passed out of limelight history but continued to be employed by the Crown. He became in turn Governor of Bermuda, Governor of Trinidad, and Governor of St. Helena. And England made him a Knight and an Admiral on the retired list.

Not long after returning to England in the fall of 1846, Elliot was sent out as *Governor and Commander-in-Chief in and over the Bermuda, alias Somers' Islands*,[2a] where he was to spend the next eight years, 1846-54.[11a] The 360 Bermudas or Somers Islands group was discovered in 1515 by Juan de Bermudez, sailing under the Spanish flag, but no settlement was made there until 1609, when Sir George Somers was wrecked on one of the sunken reefs, while conveying English colonists to Virginia. In 1612, the Virginia Company obtained a concession of the island from James I and, that same year, colonized on St. George's Island. In 1615, *The Company of the City of London for the Plantation of the Somers Islands* bought the islands from the Virginia Company for £2,000 and settled and governed the group from 1615 to 1684. Representative government was introduced into the Colony in 1620 but, in 1684, the Charter of the new body of adventurers was cancelled, the Crown took over and, from 1684, invariably appointed the governors.[13a]

Christmas 1846 found the Elliots settled in their new residence, 'Clarence Hill' in Hamilton, Bermuda, and the capital town's weekly, the *Bermuda Royal Gazette*, on 5th January 1947, published the new governor's first proclamation, dated 2nd January.[2b] His Excellency 'thought fit to continue and confirm all Persons holding Commissions within this Government in their respective Offices—until it shall by me be ordered to the contrary.' Three weeks later, on 26th January, the *Royal Gazette* announced that Governor Elliot had prorogued 'the said Colonial Parliament to 4th March 1847, of which as well the Members of the Legislative Council, as the Members of the House of Assembly.'[2c]

Soon after his arrival in the Bermudas, Elliot learned of the islanders' chief project, the deepening of the channel leading into the harbour of St. George's. Early in March 1847, he made a personal inspection of the operations in progress. The Bermudians turned out for the festive occasion and were not regretful, for the day was to prove very exciting. About noon-day, the Governor, accompanied by one Colonel Barry, a local favourite, and others of the official party, embarked at the Government Steps, Market Square, and proceeded to Paget Island to inspect the submarine explosion on the channel. The *Royal Gazette* detailed 'the inspection and clever performance of His Excellency' who, upon reaching Paget Island:

> . . . put on his woollen clothes and was conducted to the diving Hulk off the Port. On going on board he was invested by Sergeant Harris, R.S. and M., the operator, with the diving dress, and descended three times to the depth of twenty-five feet. The first time His Excellency merely examined the Shoal that was to be blasted, when he was hauled up, and on being supplied with a Canister of Gunpowder prepared for the purpose, he again descended to place it in a position for blasting. On his coming up and the Hulk removed to a careful distance from the place of explosion, the Voltaic battery was applied, but, in consequence of the wire meeting with some accident, it failed to operate. His Excellency in no wise discouraged by this untoward event, was again invested with the Helmet of descension, and being furnished with another Canister of Gunpowder he returned to the bottom, where, having placed this second canister as required, he was hauled up and the Hulk removed as before. The Battery was applied and the charge exploded which broke up immense pieces of rock, to an unusual area. The water over which required some time to settle before it could be ascertained to what extent it had removed the shoal.[2d]

Governor Elliot, having disembarked at Paget, assumed his usual dress and proceeded to Colonel Barry's residence from whence, after refreshments, he departed for 'Clarence Hill'. *The Royal Gazette* writer declared the Governor's purpose was to make:

> . . . the Harbour of St. Georges a certain and safe place of refuge for large merchant vessels in distress or otherwise; as well as for Men-of-War and Ocean Steamers of all sizes: for when this work is completed, no mariner need hesitate to approach the island: particularly now that we have so splendid a Light House in full operation, which is so highly eulogized, and which is said to have already been the means of saving several vessels from ship-wreck.[2d]

In closing, the *Gazette* writer spoke of Governor Elliot's 'perseverence (which was) evinced by him to test the progress of the work' as indicating 'an encouragement on the part of the Government's continued approbation and aid' to the Bahamas, which 'for their geographic position,—on the high road of Commerce between the Eastern and Western world—have always been a place of refuge for vessels in distress, even with their natural impediments; how much more will their utility in this particular be increased by the improvements now in progress, and doubtless will be fully carried out'. [2d]

The 23rd March edition of the *Gazette* quoted from the *New Albion* of 6th March previous a lengthy explanation 'and just meed of praise of the proceedings of our present Governor, when Minister from the court of St. James to the Republic of Texas, as given by General Houston in the Senate of the United States recently'—and which the *Bermuda Royal Gazette* felt assured would 'be perused by the inhabitants of these Islands generally and with much gratification'. [2e] The *Albion* noted that everyone, doubtless, remembered 'the obloquy, which for political purposes, was attempted to be cast on this officer (Elliot) by a portion of the press of the United States' which 'accused' Elliot 'of being the secret enemy of the United States—of meddling improperly with the negotiation going on between Texas and the cabinet at Washington'. However, recently, 'the clear sunshine of truth easily dissipates these misty accusations' and General Sam Houston, formerly President of the Republic of Texas and, now, a Senator of that state, 'has taken an opportunity of doing justice to Capt. Elliot and defending him from all and every charge made against him'. Houston had chosen, as occasion to make explanation, his speech in Congress 'on the bill for granting to the President three millions of dollars to make peace with Mexico'. The *Gazette* quoted the *New York Albion* as having copied its 'remarks from *The Congressional Globe* of the 19th ult.' which recorded that:

> Genl. Houston said, while he was on this branch of the subject, he would here, in his place, state some matters in relation to things which had been much discussed at large. Texas, to be sure, had great domestic misfortunes, but she was never recreant to the principles of liberty; and if she had stood alone from, and been disregarded and denounced by all the nations of the earth, she would never have swerved from the principles of constitutional liberty. She never could have been driven from the principles engrafted in the very nature of her constituency. She never thought of forming an alliance which could have dishonoured her escutcheon. She never thought of owning allegiance to any country but one with which she could be incorporated on principles of equality. —Texas never thought of making any of the institutions she had taken to that country, or to impair her self respect, or the respect of other nations. England never made a suggestion to Texas, which, if she had pursued or accepted, would have degraded her in the eyes of the purest patriot that ever lived. Nothing was ever proposed or done but what ought to take place between nations, although the journals of the United States, on various occasions, had thought fit to assail, not only the authorities of Texas, but the British and other foreign Ministers, and to denounce them as foreign emissaries, and the President of the Republic of Texas as traitor to the principles of liberty, for which he ought to be hurled

from his estate. He was perfectly aware that all this would cause some excitement, which might lead to annexation; but Texas was not in a very comfortable position; and therefore he was willing that the United States should be induced to act by public opinion.

So far, then, as that was concerned, he did not regret the abuse which was heaped on Texas by the people of the United States, and by some statesmen too. But England was represented by a gentleman (Capt. Elliot) whose intelligence would compare with that of any representative from any country, if Mr. H. was able to judge. He was a man who sympathised with Texas, and he proposed nothing but what was for the interest of Texas. He was representing faithfully his own Government, and he regretted that the blind zeal of Mexico could have withstood the strong remonstrances which had been made to her to recognize the independence of Texas. He required nothing but commercial relations between England and Texas, and an interchange of her fabrics for the products of the south. The character of that gentleman was pre-eminently praiseworthy and patriotic, and it would seem that Texas appreciates him when she writes her annals. And as a statesman and diplomatist, he was entitled to all the respect and gratitude of Texas.[2e]

An extra edition of the *Gazette*, 21st April 1847, announced that on that day Governor Elliot 'took his seat on the throne and heard the President of the Council, in the Colonial Legislature assembled, welcome him and concur with his suggestions'.[2f] After courtesies and praise to his predecessor, Elliot recommended to the renewed consideration of the Legislature such matters as 'the subject of religious and useful education for the Youth of the Colony', which, continued the Governor, 'all classes of people' find 'so necessary for the common contentment, and for inculcating a becoming sense of the rights and responsibilities of freemen'. To this claim, Elliot encouraged 'a systematic mode of affording the public aid and encouragement to this object'. Next, he called notice to an Imperial Act which, 'since your last Session has been received, and will be laid before you, extending to the Colonial Legislatures complete fiscal authority'; the Governor added that he hoped the Legislature could 'make adequate provision for the service of the ensuing year without increasing the public burdens'. With pleasure, Elliot reported that 'the Board of Ordnance had abated the charge for Gunpowder in the Works proceeding at the Eastern and Western entrances of Saint George's', and 'that the important work at the mouth of Saint George's Harbour has been materially advanced'. As to other public works, the Governor advocated 'the establishment of a School for Engineering and general scientific attainment, and the commencement of a Mechanics' Institute'. In addition, Elliot requested the Legislature's notice to 'the advantage that the Colony might derive from the instruction of some few of our own people in the art of submarine blasting', because 'the whole North Coast of these Islands is almost devoid of places of refuge for the boats in the sudden Northerly gales of the Winter season' and, 'from personal observation', Elliot was satisfied 'that several of these inlets could be rendered practicable for them at all times of tide, by sub-marine blasting, at a moderate expense'. Praising 'the Seamen of Bermuda', the Governor said that the Legislature should deem it 'an object worthy of your patriotism to foster and incite their genius by procuring for them, all available instruction in every branch of science tending to increase the Maritime advantages of the Islands, and the Security of the people engaged in the fisheries and the coasting intercourse'. Aware of the numerous opinions and difficulties surrounding the question of emigration from Europe, Governor Elliot hoped the Bermudian Legislature would 'think fit to pass an Act uniting the functions of an Immigration to an Agricultural Committee, extend their powers, render them Trustees for the application of the fund already existing for the introduction of Gardeners, Artisans, and Farm and other Servants make a small addition to that vote and appropriate a moderate compensation for an active and intelligent Secretary' because, Elliot continued, such a system was in operation at the Cape of Good Hope, where much 'cautious yet satisfactory progress' on the very important emigration concern had been realized. Perhaps, surmised Elliot, '60 or 70 (emigrants) could be introduced into Bermuda for less than £100'. In closing, the Governor congratulated the industrious islanders and offered thanks to God for the promising appearance of the crops, gardens, orchards, and pasturage in the islands and, concurring with 'experienced persons on the necessity for vigorous and steadily maintained efforts to clear and cultivate the land', the Governor noted 'that the positions in the world are few, and the circumstances rare, in which a small but energetic Community may find a more varied field for their skill and industry, fruition with less painful toil, a larger exemption of the dispiriting anxieties of life, a more powerful protection on its secure enjoyment'. The *Gazette* noted with pleasure that Mrs Elliot attended the session to hear her husband's speech.[2f]

Early in May 1847, Elliot's *Message on the Subject of Education* was laid before the House of Assembly and recommended a law authorizing the appointment of a Committee on Education to 'promote religious and useful Education amongst the Youth of the Colony; the purchase, rent, building, or repair of School Houses, the supply of School apparatus and the payment of Teacher's Salaries';[2g] a yearly and detailed census of children between the ages of four and 16 years; that the 'Committee be required to grant aid on equal principles to all Schools';[2g] and that the 'Committee should report twice a year to the Governor and Council for presentation to the Legislature' and, owing to 'the isolation of this small Colony and the difficulty of procuring Teachers', the Governor advocated the establishment of 'a good Normal School here', in the islands, which 'should be established on a principle which may best enable the Ministers of all persuasions to foster it by their zeal for the spread of Christian Educations'. [2g] With his *Message on Education*, Elliot enclosed some educational publications which he had procured from the British and Foreign School Library.

In July, the Governor received a letter, dated Downing Street, 17th June 1847, from Secretary of State Lord Grey, in which the Governor was asked to thank the Bermudians for their gracious gift of £500 sterling 'for the relief of the destitute in Ireland, Scotland, or in any other part of the United Kingdom'. The 20th July *Bermuda Royal Gazette*, with pride, published Grey's letter to Governor Elliot. [2h]

In his address to the House of Assembly, 15th January 1850, Governor Elliot summoned the legislators' attention to the need for 'the virtous and industrious training of the youth' of the colony; his gathering of information 'from persons of better local experience', his subsequent 'conviction that the condition indispensable to the accelerated progress of the Colony is the systematic encouragement of the intelligence and industry of the people, particularly in those pursuits suited to our climate and situation', and, consequently, his hope 'that the late small immigration from Madeira may be the means of restoring, or creating amongst us valuable processes'—that the Portuguese 'export large quantities of excellent wine, and with due instruction it would be spiritless indeed to doubt that the English race, settled in Islands on the same parallel and with a like climate, should be unable, sooner or later to achieve similar results at all events to some extent'. [1a]

A fortnight later, on 1st February, the Assembly Secretary recorded in the House Proceedings that, after several years' effort, Governor Elliot had secured from Downing Street both permission and funds for an insular improvement long dear to Bermudian hearts. An amount of £2,416 was allowed for the purpose 'of erecting a Causeway with connecting Bridges between St. George's and the main Island' in order 'to afford the Colony the convenience of this means of communications'. For this project, Lord Grey suggested that Governor Elliot propose to the Colonial Legislature the use of convict labour. [1b]

Along the lighter vein, His Excellency's proclivities at yachting fill many columns of the *Gazette*. In the spring of 1847, the Governor personally awarded the Yachting Club's cup at the annual and lavish festivity upon which occasion he reminded the gay crowd that he trusted such festivity would not be 'looked to as a precedent' as he felt it 'might deter members of moderate means from attempting to win a Cup', and, also, because he felt such a Club should afford not only 'rational and exhilirating amusement, and social recreation and enjoyment amongst the Gentlemen of all professions, but because he considered the establishment of such a Club as leading to higher and more desirable results', such as 'encouragement to improvement in building, and also to those employed in navigating the Yachts, and was congenial to the spirit of a great Naval Nation'. [21]

Elliot's second insular governorship was Trinidad off the coast of Venezuela, near Guiana, where, a generation before, he had served as Protector of Slaves. The years 1854-56 found him serving as *Governor and Commander-in-Chief in and over Trinidad Island and its Dependencies*, successor at that post to George Francis Robert Lord Harris,[5a] and appointed by the Duke of Newcastle, Secretary for War and the Colonies.[14a]

Trinidad was discovered by Columbus on Trinity Sunday, 1498. Its colonization by Spain began about 1532 but proceeded with but little progress. In 1595, Sir Walter Raleigh 'arrived at Trinidad' and, 'casting anchor at Point Curiapan, which the Spaniards called Punto de Gallo', destroyed the Spanish settlements and claimed the island for England. [15a] Of his conquest, Raleigh wrote:

> The island of Trinidad hath the form of a sheep-hook, and is but narrow and will bear sugar, ginger, or any other commodity that the Indies yield, even gold which the Spaniards confessed that they found grains of in some of the rivers.[15b]

Even in 1595, Raleigh called Trinidad an island 'of divers nations' [15c] and so it continued until 1783, when its many nationalities were further increased because Spain offered 'foreigners of all nations' unusual advantages to settle there, provided they professed the Roman Catholic religion. The result was a large increase in population, including many refugees from the French Revolution, driven from Santo Domingo and other parts. During the war with Spain in 1797, Trinidad was occupied by the British and held as a military conquest until 1802, when it was ceded to England by the Treaty of Amiens.[15b]

By mid-19th century and Elliot's Trinidad governorship, 1854-56, the island was wedded to sugar production and had suffered the usual West Indian plantation and emancipation story. Elliot's predecessor, Governor Lord Harris, had, during his administration, 1846-54, reported to England that not only had Trinidad, since 1838, the year when freedom was fully granted, shown 'no net profit' to her estate owners but 'there has been a dead loss of British Capital to the amount of at least £1,000,000 sterling'.[14b] The next year, 1849, the Government had despatched the Alexander-Candler visit of investigation of British West Indian experience but, even by 1854 and Elliot's arrival in Trinidad, auxiliary measures were sadly neglected.[16a] Governor Harris had been responsible, since the emancipists refused to work, for the introduction of East Indian labour[4a] and, upon arriving in this Trinidadian's wrangle,[5a] Elliot's position was further complicated by local religious agitation. The story was retold in a special centenary edition of the *Port-of-Spain Gazette* which recalled:

> In 1854 we find a Governor incited by sectarian friends refusing to recognise a Catholic Archbishop (the Right Reverent Dr. Spaccapietra) sent from Rome because he was a foreigner, and a consequential agitation of some bitterness followed. Naturally petitions reached the Throne, claiming for the Catholics of Trinidad the rights guaranteed to them by the Capitulation. The result was inevitable, and the Governor received a dispatch calling upon him to recognize as head of the Catholic Church in the colony any prelate presenting credentials from Rome whom the Catholics would recognise as such. It was during the regime of Sir Arthur Gordon that the discriminating Ecclesiatical Ordinance was repealed; religious equality re-established and the land-laws really reformed, whilst secondary education was also dealt with more in accordance with the wishes of the people.[18]

Immediately upon arrival, Governor Elliot turned his attention to alleviating the colony's 'extraordinary expenses incurred during the late visitation of Cholera', [4b] and to the authorization of 'the erection of Public Washing Houses within the Town of Port of Spain'. [5b] His first proclamation announced that the ordinances of the previous administration 'have been allowed and confirmed by Her Majesty, and their Honours the Judges of the said Colony, and the several Magistrates therein and all others concerned are to take notice and govern themselves accordingly', namely:

1. . . . An Ordinance No. 3 for the better Government of Chinese Immigrants introduced at the public expense.

2. . . . An Ordinance No. 8 to extend the Sittings of the Supreme Civil Court in Equity.

3. . . . An Ordinance No. 10 for the regulation of Municipal Corporations in this Island.

4. . . . An Ordinance No. 11 for securing to Alexander Williams Anderson the exclusive benefit for a limited time of a certain discovery in the manufacture of Sugar.

5. . . . An Ordinance No. 12 for the granting of Writs of Habeas Corpus.

6. . . . An Ordinance No. 13 for regulating the Printing and Publishing of Newspapers.

7. . . . An Ordinance No. 14 to make provision for defraying those expenses of the Government of this Colony for the year one thousand and eight hundred and fifty-four, of which the amount is not already fixed, or the payment not duly authorized.

8. . . . An Ordinance No. 15 for facilitating the transmission of monies through the Post Office, and for the registration of Letters.

9. . . . An Ordinance No. 16 to authorize the employment of Convicts at hard labour beyond the precincts of the Royal Gaol.

10. . . . An Ordinance No. 17 for the better regulation of Hucksters and Pedlars in the Rural Districts of this Colony.

11. . . . An Ordinance No. 18 to repeal certain Duties of Customs and to raise other duties in lieu thereof.

12. . . . An Ordinance No. 19 to alter the duty on Rum and other Spirits.

13. . . . An Ordinance No. 20 for facilitating the sale of Lands adjudicated to Her Majesty for default of payment of Ward Rates.[5c]

In the 12th April 1854 weekly edition of the *Trinidad Royal Gazette*, Governor Elliot quoted for the islanders from Newcastle's Despatch, dated 18th February, in which Newcastle had received 'Lord Harris's despatch of the 20th of December last, No. 143, transmitting the report of the Industrial Exhibition held in Trinidad in January 1853 and, from which, Downing Street felt that such Exhibitions are likely to be productive of the greatest good to the Colony' and trusted 'that the Colonists will not allow Lord Harris' zealous efforts to establish them to be thrown away'. [5d] The same *Gazette* carried the Governor's Ordinance 'enacted by and with the advice and consent of the Council of Government thereof', for 'defraying the Expenses of the Government of this Colony for the year 1854', such as:

Revenue Services	Fifty Pounds.
Administration of Justice	Two Hundred and Fifty Pounds.
Ecclesiastical	Two Hundred and Fifty Pounds.
Education	Five Hundred Pounds.
Hospitals	Three Thousand Seven Hundred and Fifty Pounds.
Police	One Thousand Four Hundred Pounds.
Gaols	Two Thousand Pounds.
Rent (Public Houses)	Two Thousand One Hundred and Sixty Pounds.
Transport	One Hundred Pounds.
Conveyance of Mails	One Thousand Three Hundred Pounds.
Postage	One Thousand and Six Hundred Pounds.
Repairs	Three Thousand One Hundred and Twenty Pounds.
Road, Streets, and Bridges ...	Four Thousand Five Hundred Pounds.

Miscellaneous Services	One Thousand Seven Hundred and Seventy Pounds.
Interest	Seven Thousand Nine Hundred Pounds.
Immigration...	Nineteen Thousand Pounds.
Drawbacks and Refund of Duties...	Three Thousand Pounds.
Sinking Fund	Six Thousand Three Hundred and Seventy-Five Pounds.[5e]

A Londoner, Arthur Auckland Leopold Cochrane, interested Elliot in his claims as the inventor of a process 'for certain improvements in the use of the Bitumen of this Colony (Trinidad) in the manufacture of Fuel', which invention Cochrane believed to be of great public utility. Soon, the Governor's Ordinance secured to Cochrane 'the exclusive benefit for a limited time of a certain Invention in manufacturing Fuel'.[5f] At the same time, a gubernatorial ordinance secured 'to Alexander Williams Anderson the exclusive benefit for a limited time of a certain discovery in the manufacture of sugar".'[5g]

The *Trinidad Royal Gazette* for 10th May 1854 published the Queen's 29th March declaration of war against the Emperor of all the Russians.[5h] At the same issue, Governor Elliot's proclamation explained Her Majesty's desire 'to lessen as much as possible' the evil of the war with Russia and, thereby, Her Majesty's order that Russian vessels 'in any ports or places in Her Majesty's Indian territories, under the Government of the East India Company, or within any of Her Majesty's foreign or colonial possessions, shall be allowed thirty days from the publication of this Order in such Indian territories, or foreign or colonial possessions, for loading their cargoes and departing from such ports or places'. Though[5h] the Crimean war did not directly concern Trinidadian affairs, two years passed before Queen Victoria's Proclamation of 28th April 1856, which was the occasion, a month later, in Trinidad, of a special and extra edition of the *Gazette*. 'A Definite Treaty of Peace and Friendship between Us and Our Allies and His Imperial Majesty the Emperor of all the Russias' was announced as having been 'concluded at Paris on the Thirtieth of March last', and the publication of the same 'throughout all Our Dominions' to 'all Our loving Subjects' was commanded and these loving Subjects were to observe the treaty 'inviolably, as well by Sea as by Land'.[5i] Several weeks later, Governor Elliot's 'Proclamation for A Public Thanksgiving to Almighty God' for the restoration of peace provided for observations throughout the island colony on 29th June 1856.[5j]

In 1854, Elliot proceeded with the division of the Colony of Trinidad into Divisions, Counties, Districts and Wards and directed and proclaimed 'that the Chaguaramas Ward shall henceforth consist of the Quarter of

Chaguaramas — the Islands of ChacaChacare — Momos — Gasparillo — Begorrat and Long' and 'the Ward of Cedros shall consist of the Quarters of Cedros—Irois and Erin'.[5k] Elliot, in each island Governorship, secured the establishment of a public library and vested certain lands, buildings and hereditaments in trustees, for purposes of the Church.

Soon after being sworn in as Governor of Trinidad, Elliot had 'called for reports on the miscellaneous statistics of the island such as taxes and duties, revenue and expenditure, military expenditure, public works, legislation, the political franchise, pensions, ecclesiastical returns, education, coins and exchanges, imports and exports, agriculture and manufacturing, grants of land, gaols and prisoners, charitable institutions, and shipping'.[6a] Throughout his two-year term, he was receiving and reviewing these various statistical reports and interviewing and appointing such local officials as the Inspector of Police,[5l] Inspectors of Weights and Measures,[5l] Wardens,[5m] Stipendiary County Magistrates,[5m] Justices of the Peace,[5n] Hospital Medical Superintendents, minor colonial postal officials, Agents General of Immigrants, County Supervisors,[5n] Receiver General,[5o] Harbour Masters, Colonial Postmaster, Government Messengers, the Private Secretary to the Governor (John Scott Bushe),[5o] the Revising Barrister,[5p] the Inspector of Schools, and the Inspector of Prisons.[5p]

With pride, the *Trinidad Royal Gazette* of 20th June 1855, and of 27th August, 1856, quoted honours for the island's governor, namely:

The London Gazette,
8th May, 1855.

Admiralty, 5th May, 1855, Captain Charles Elliot to be Rear-Admiral on the Reserved Half Pay List.[5n]

Then, the next year, 1856, and again, from:

The London Gazette,
Tuesday, 22nd July, 1856.

War Department,
July 19, 1856.

The Queen has been graciously pleased to give orders for the appointment of Rear-Admiral Charles Elliot, Governor and Commander-in-Chief in and over the Island of Trinidad, to be an Ordinary Member of the Civil Division of the Second Class or Knight Commander of the Most Honourable Order of the Bath.[5q]

At the close of 1856, Sir Charles Elliot was returned to England. On 15th January 1862, he became a vice-admiral[11a] and, early in 1863, was appointed to succeed Sir E. H. Drummond Hay as Governor of tiny St.

Helena, in the South Atlantic Ocean. There, he was to pass six long years, the same number as Napoleon, from 1815 to 1821. The Governor was paid by the Colonial Office an 'annual salary in British or army sterling of £2,000' and allowed Government House for his personal residence.[8a]

St. Helena, 1,200 miles from the west coast of South Africa and 800 from the island of Ascension, was discovered by Juan de Nova Castella, a Portuguese navigator, on St. Helens's Day, 11st May 1502. The Portuguese built a church on the isle but made no permanent settlement, and they kept their discovery a secret from other European nations until 1588, when Captain Cavendish, the English adventurer and third circumnavigator of the globe, sailed into St. Helena's waters. The Dutch held the island from 1645 to 1650 and then abandoned the desolate place. Then, the East India Company took possession and was confirmed in its holding by charters granted in 1651 and 1673, the Dutch meanwhile having twice seized the island and been expelled, in 1665 and, again, in 1673. Excepting for the six-year period of Napoleon's imprisonment there, 1815-21, St. Helena remained under the East India Company until April 1834, when it came under the direct government of the Crown. The 'natives' and population of the isle, with the exception of a few English families, were, by 1863, when Elliot began his six-year governorship, sprung from the intermixture of East Indians, Chinese, Malayans, and Africans, in the days of slavery, with English settlers, soldiers, sailors, and other Europeans.

Immediately upon arrival at St. Helena, Elliot, duly sworn in,[7a] called for the recent (1861) census of the island which showed the following figures for the 47 square miles of the island:

	Whites		Coloured		Total	
	Males	Females	Males	Females	Males	Females
Jamestown	817	821	738	892	1,555	1,713
Country ...	598	641	457	532	1,055	1,173
Garrison ...	—	—	—	—	760	188
Total [8b]	1,415	1,462	1,195	1,424	3,370	3,074

This census showed that St. Helena had 109 paupers and 25 emigrants [8c] and that the Jamestown gaol was capable of containing 16 persons who usually were 'felons or thieves'. [8d]

Jamestown itself, had one hospital, one lunatic asylum, one almshouse, and several small churches, all Church of England with the exception of one Baptist;[8e] the education of the island's youths was in the hands of the church.[8f] The town boasted two weekly newspapers: the *St. Helena Guardian* printed 200 copies each week, and the *St. Helena Spectator*, 120 copies.[8g] The island fisheries, chiefly mackerel and albicore, were valued in sterling at probably £4,000 per annum and were consumed by the islanders.[8h] Imports were a great variety of products.[8i] Exports were chiefly guano, whale oil, hides and horns.[8j]

Elliot conscientiously interviewed each individual applicant for the numerous colonial gubernatorial appointments.[8k] Hudson R. Janick received the position of Colonial Secretary, Auditor, and Superintendent of Post Office at £650 per annum.[8k] Among other appointees were wharf watchman, engineers, Board of Health officer and assistants, Savings Bank manager, teachers, Supreme Court Chief Justice, Coroner, Crier, the Police Magistrate and various prison and gaol officers, and such various militia as the quartermaster, surgeon, adjutant, chargé-of-arms, and orderlies.[8k]

Governor Elliot's 1867 report [8l] to the Colonial Office gives a clear picture of the value of the exports and imports of the little island:

United Kingdom—Imports therefrom, £50,310 [8m]

Exports thereto,   £5,606 [8m]

BRITISH COLONIES

	Imports therefrom	Exports thereto
Calcutta	4,372	
Australia	284	
Akyab (Burma)	1,545	
Mauritius	2,843	
Penang	2,387	
Cape of Good Hope ...	27,037	1,266
Total[8n]...	38,468	1,266

FOREIGN COUNTRIES

	Imports therefrom	Exports thereto
Arabia	195	245
Africa West Coast... ...	732	
France	655	
Hamburg	7	

Holland	...	...	...	III	
Japan	...	...	...	36	
Java	...	...	...	2,109	
Manila	...	...	...	282	
Russia	...	...	...	110	
Southern Whale Fishery	...			19,576	
Trustan da Cunha	...		...	31	
United States	...		...	1,557	21,910
Rio de Janeiro	...		...		21
Total[8n]	...		...	25,381	22,176

The consideration of land claims and the granting of land consumed much of Elliot's and the Council's time.[7b] Elliot's horticultural interest expressed itself in his efforts to establish the chinchona plant trees on the island, 1868-69, at the several chinchona plantations and at the Public Nursery.[8o]

On 12th September 1865, Elliot became Admiral,[11a] and, in 1869, he retired and returned to England, to live for the years remaining to him. Perchance he never wrote his memoirs though, at St. Helena in his sixties, surely he had ample leisure and unquestionably he had an uncommonly bitter-sweet and rich cargo of reminiscences. Thirty-nine when he conducted England's war against China, in his early forties when he strove to steady the Texas Republic as an independent ship, Elliot was 74 when, on 9th September 1875, at Witteycombe, Exeter,[17a] he departed into history and life eternal.

BIBLIOGRAPHY & REFERENCES

MICROFILM

BERMUDA

1 C.O.R. 40/41. Sessional Papers, 1850-54, Legislative Council; Assembly.
a p.57ff; b p.79.
2 C.O.R. 41. Newspapers, item 2, 1844-47.
a p.310; b p.301; c p.316; d p.327; e p.329; f p.333B; g p.342; h p.363; i p.335.
3 *Royal Gazette* and *Bermuda Commercial and General Advertiser and Recorder*.
Item 3, 1848-53, ditto.
Item 4, 1847-51, *Bermuda Herald*.
Item 5, 1847-51, *The Bermudian*.

TRINIDAD

4 C.O.R. 298, items 26 through 28, Legislative Council; Executive Council.
   a 298/28, p.6off; *b* 298/28, p.79.
5 C.O.R. 299, items 7 and 8, Government Gazettes.
   299/7: *a* p.392; *b* p.428; *c* p.396; *d* p.409; *e* p.401; *f* p.406; *g* p.427, *h* p.416.
   299/8: *i* p.354; *j* p.372; *k* p.7; *l* p.88; *m* p.71; *n* p.99; *o* p.185; *p* p.200; *q* p.435.
6 C.O.R. 300, items 65 through 67, Blue Books of Statistics.
   300/65: *a* pp.1-265.
   300/66: *b* pp.1-159.
   300/67: *c* pp.1-156.

ST HELENA

7 C.O.R. 250, item 4, Sessional Papers, 1860–80, Legislative Council.
   a p.22; *b* p.24.
8 C.O.R. 252, items 28 through 34, Blue Books of Statistics, Miscellaneous.
   252/32: *b* p.144; *c* p.70; *d* p.121ff; *e* p.131; *f* p.156ff; *g* p.162; *h* p.118; *i* p.84; *j* p.96.
   252/33: *a* p.44; *k* p.45ff; *l* p.81ff; *m* p.82; *n* p. 83; *o* p.230.

PRINTED

9 Brooke, T. H., *A History of the Island of St Helena from Its Discovery by the Portuguese to the Year* 1806. London: Black, Parry and Kingsbury, 1808.
10 Coke, Thomas, *A History of the West Indies containing the Natural, Civil, and Ecclesiastical History of Each Island; with an Account of the Missions Instituted in those Islands, from the Commencement of their Civilisation; but more especially of the Missions which have been established in that Archipelago by the Society Late in Connexion with the Rev. John Wesley.* 3 vols. Liverpool: Nuttall, Fisher, and Dixon, 1808.
11 Laughton, K. J. 'Elliot', *Dictionary of National Biography*, ed. Leslie Stephen, Vol. XVII. London: Smith, Elder and Company, 1889.
   a p.251.
12 Spruner-Menke, *Hand-Atlas fur Die Geschichte des Mittelalters und Der Neueren Zeit.* Gotha: Justus Perthes, 1880.
13 Pascoe, *Two Hundred Years of the S.P.G.*, 1701–1900.
   a p.102ff; *b* p.208ff.
14 Bell and Morrell, *Select Documents on British Colonial Policy*, 1830–1860.
   a p.428; *b* p.429ff.
15 Ralegh, *The Discoverie of Guiana.*
   a p.11; *b* p.13; *c* p.14.
16 Annie Heloise Abel and Frank J. Klingberg (eds.), *A Side-Light on Anglo-American Relations, 1839–1858.* Lancaster, Pennsylvania: The Association for the Study of Negro Life and History, Incorporated, 1927.
   a p.236ff.

NEWSPAPERS

17 London *The Times*, 15th September, 1875.
   a p.7, col. d, Obituary.
18 *Port-of-Spain Gazette*, 21st September, 1925, No. 13, 911, Vol. XLVIII, Trinidad. Library of Congress, Washington.

Index

INDEX